AERIAL SILKS:
91 WAYS TO SPLIT ON SILKS

BY: SAM MELLOR

PHOTOS: SAM MELLOR
MODEL: MARIVI VALDEZ

ALL RIGHTS RESERVED.
NO PART OF THIS PUBLICATION MAY BE REPRODUCED, STORED IN A RETRIEVAL SYSTEM, OR TRANSMITTED IN ANY WAY OR BY ANY MEANS, ELECTRONIC, MECHANICAL, PHOTOCOPYING, RECORDING OR OTHERWISE, WITHOUT THE PRIOR WRITTEN PERMISSION BY
SAM MELLOR.

IT IS RECOMMENDED THAT YOU CHECK WITH YOUR DOCTOR OR HEALTHCARE PROVIDER BEFORE BEGINNING NEW EXERCISE PROGRAMS.

WHILST EVERY CARE HAS BEEN TAKEN IN PREPARATION OF THIS MATERIAL, THERE IS A REAL CHANCE OF INJURY IN EXECUTION OF THE MOVEMENTS DESCRIBED IN THIS BOOK. THE PUBLISHERS AND ALL PERSONS INVOLVED IN THE MAKING OF THIS BOOK WILL NOT ACCEPT RESPONSIBILITY FOR INJURY TO ANY DEGREE, INCLUDING DEATH, TO ANY PERSON AS A RESULT OF PARTICIPATION IN THE ACTIVITIES DESCRIBED IN THIS MANUAL. PURCHASE OR USE OF THIS DOCUMENT CONSTITUES AGREEMENT TO THIS EFFECT. FURTHERMORE, RIGGING OF AERIAL EQUIPMENT IS NOT DISCUSSED IN THIS MANUAL. CONSULT A PROFESSIONAL RIGGER WHEN IT COMES TO USING ANY HANGING OR AERIAL EQUIPMENT.

PUBLISHED BY: KINDLE DIRECT PUBLISHING

UNITED STATES OF AMERICA

ISBN: 9781708777784

FORWARD

Thank you for purchasing! Two years ago I had an idea, and after many sleepless nights and multiple kids later this reference book was finally born! A visual record of all my favorite split poses! These poses are sectioned into categories based on the type of entry and have brief picture guides as well as descriptions. While I do cover alot of bases, remember this is not meant to be a full tutorial book but a visual reference guide to remind intermediate/advanced aerialists about tips/tricks/entries to poses they have already practiced with a coach/spotter. Base skills such as inversions, footlocks and belays are used commonly in these poses but are not included in the picture guides. Pay heed to the warnings and quick tips as any pose, no matter how simple, can be dangerous and cause injury.

DISCLAIMER

- I did not create the poses listed here. This is a culmination of poses learned throughout my career from various resources. I am merely a humble student and lover of the arts and decided it was time to put everything down on paper!
- There are many ways to enter into some of these poses, I have chosen to display my favorite entries.
- The model used is an advanced level aerialist and very talented, some of these poses are not as easy as they appear.
- Names for poses vary greatly from studio to studio, the names I use are the ones most common to me.
- Remember that all of these poses can be DANGEROUS and should only be performed with coaches, mats and proper rigging set up.
- This guide is meant to be a partner to your training and a reminder of steps to those who have a consistent practice. It is never recommend to learn new material without a coach or proper safety in play.
- Support your local studios! I will constantly recommend getting a private from your local coach, they are the heart and soul of aerial. They dedicate and sacrifice alot to bring the best knowledge and safety to your fingertips.

KEY TERMS

REMINDER: Reminds you of the general cautions and care you need to take one performing the poses.

tip: Covers important information needed to complete the poses properly. Also provides information to help troubleshoot certain poses.

⚠️: Warns of poses that have extremely easy potential to fall out of. Please understand ALL poses have the potential to be fall out poses. However poses marked with this sign should be taken with extreme caution.

VIEW FLIP: You will see this in some of the picture diagrams. This symbolizes that model has flipped and the pose is now being shown from the opposite angle. (Back to Front / Front to Back)

SFL (RSFL/LSFL) Denotes a Single Footlock. R and L referring to right versus left single footlock.

DFL (RDFL/LDFL) Denotes a Double Footlock. R and L referring to right versus left double footlock.

As you go through this guide, remember that every body is different and responds to the poses in different ways. Some aerialists weaknesses are others strengths and vice versa. Pay attention to your body and do not fret if your pose does not look exactly as the poses do in this guide. Varying degrees in flexibility, strength and even silk stretchiness can cause changes in the end pose appearance. Special thanks to Marivi Valdez, the beautiful model for this book, you can find her on instagram @mariflyin!

Do not let your ego get the best of you, new poses should only be performed with an instructor/spotter present and with the proper safety measures! Always warm up and never force yourself into a position. Don't forget to take care of your gear and body by removing any jewelry before practicing!

Overall, practice with intelligence, respect the silk and let your body be your guide!

HAPPY SILKING!
-SAM MELLOR

Tag us in your poses!
We love to see the outcomes!

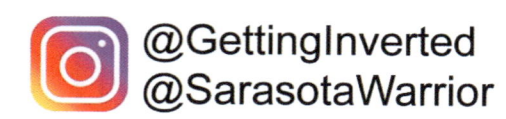

@GettingInverted
@SarasotaWarrior

Sam Mellor
Getting Inverted

www.GettingInverted.com

TABLE OF CONTENTS

CHAPTER ONE
DOUBLE FOOTLOCK POSES
PG 1

pg 2

pg 2

pg 3

pg 4

pg 5

pg 7

pg 9

pg 12

pg 14

pg 16

pg 17

pg 19

pg 20

CHAPTER TWO
SINGLE FOOTLOCK POSES
PG 21

pg 23

pg 23

pg 24

pg 25

pg 26

pg 27

pg 28

pg 29

pg 30

pg 31

pg 34

pg 35

pg 36

pg 38

pg 39

pg 41

pg 42

pg 43

pg 44

pg 46

CHAPTER THREE
SFL + FREE POLE / WRIST WRAP POSES
PG 47

pg 48

pg 49

pg 50

pg 51

pg 53

pg 55

pg 56

pg 58

pg 60

pg 61

pg 62

pg 63

CHAPTER FOUR
INVERSION ENTRY POSES
PG 64

pg 66
pg 68
pg 70
pg 71
pg 72
pg 73
pg 74
pg 77
pg 79
pg 81
pg 82
pg 83
pg 84
pg 86
pg 88
pg 90
pg 91
pg 92
pg 93
pg 94
pg 96
pg 98
pg 99
pg 100

CHAPTER FIVE
BELAY LOOP POSES
PG 101

pg 102
pg 103
pg 104
pg 105
pg 106
pg 107
pg 108
pg 109
pg 110
pg 111
pg 112
pg 113
pg 114
pg 116

CHAPTER SIX
MISCELLANEOUS POSES
PG 117

pg 118
pg 120
pg 121
pg 122
pg 124
pg 125
pg 126
pg 128

CHAPTER ONE
POSES FROM DOUBLE FOOTLOCKS

Welcome to Chapter One! This section includes a list of all my favorite poses that stem from Double Footlocks! Remember to use this book as a guide and never by itself. You should always have a competent instructor present. Below is a quick image reference of the 13 main poses covered in this section (variations not pictured).

pg 2
pg 2
pg 3
pg 4
pg 5
pg 7
pg 9
pg 12
pg 14
pg 16
pg 17
pg 19
pg 20

pg 1

1. FRONT SPLIT

IN DOUBLE FOOTLOCK

1. Keep hips facing forward.
2. Lower with both hands before switching to a single hand hold.

2. MIDDLE SPLIT

IN DOUBLE FOOTLOCK

1. Keep hips facing forward.
2. Keep your knees facing upward.
3. Lower with both hands first before switching to a single hand hold.

REMINDER:

Even the most basic of split poses can be dangerous.
Warm up and stretch so you don't pull a muscle!

3. INCLINE SPLIT
FORWARD FACING YOUR LIFTED LEG

1. Perform footlocks one at a time.
2. Your front splitting footlock should be higher than your back leg footlock.
3. Lower with both hands before switching to single hand grip.
4. Keep your hips facing your forward raised footlock.

3a. INCLINE SPLIT
FORWARD FACING YOUR LOWER LEG

1. Perform footlocks one at a time.
2. Your back splitting footlock should be higher than your front leg footlock.
3. Lower with both hands before switching to single hand grip.
4. Keep your hips facing your front lowered footlock.

REMINDER:

Incline splits call for an increase and both legs and back flexibility! Having an oversplit on the floor is a great pre-requisiste

4. STAG SPLIT

FORWARD FACING WITH A RAISED FRONT LEG

1. Start in a forward facing split. (pg 3)
2. Bend both knees at either a 90 or 120 degree angle.

> 💬 tip
>
> To achieve this look, model started in a forward facing INCLINE split. The same shape will not be achieved in a regular level split.

4a. STAG SPLIT

REAR FACING A RAISED BACK LEG

1. Start in a rear facing incline split. (pg 3)
2. Bend both knees at either a 90 or 120 degree angle.

> 💬 tip
>
> Model's pose started as a rear facing INCLINE split. While you can perform this in a level split, it will not achieve the same shape visually.

REMINDER:
Stag splits call for an increase and both legs and back flexibility!

5. SPLIT ROLL UP
FROM A DOUBLE FOOTLOCK

1. Start in a right leg front split. (pg 2)
2. Hold front pole with both hands.
3. Look over right shoulder and begin to turn to your right with your upper body.
4. Lift and kick your right leg up between the poles.
5. Continue to bring your right leg through the poles and land back in a front split.
6. Repeat this roll up 1, 2 or 3 times depending on your comfort level!

tip

1. It's easy to lose the front footlock when bringing the leg through the poles. Keep the fabric between your front footlock and your hand grip extremely taught to try to avoid this.
2. If performing multiple roll throughs, keep an eye on the fabric twisting up your back leg. (shown as model's left back leg) Do not let the fabric wrap above your knee.

REMINDER:

Split roll up requires extra body awareness, strength and it is very easy to get tangled up if not practiced with this pose. TO EXIT: Complete the roll in reverse.

pg 5

5a. ROLL UP VARIATION
F2H – FOOT TO HEAD

A simple but beautiful variation of split roll up is the F2H variation (Foot to Head). This is a term I will use throughout the book to describe variations that enhance your split pose aesthetic.

1. Start in a split roll up [pg 5]
2. Hold the back pole with both hands.
3. Allow your back knee to bend, drop your head back and arch your spine.

tip Pulling your shoulder blades together and pushing your chest forward will also help to increase your backbend range in this pose.

REMINDER: Note that F2H poses require an increased flexibility beyond a basic split pose. Please remember to warm up and stretch well before diving into any pose in this book!

6. TEARDROP
FROM A DOUBLE FOOTLOCK

1. Start in a right dominant split roll up. (pg 5)
2. Place your left arm high, slide your right arm between the pole of the fabric and your body.

RIGHT ARM THROUGH

RIGHT FOOT IN FRONT

DO NOT let go with your left hand until you have this grip.

3. Regrip the pole with your right arm by twisting and reaching across your body.

RIGHT ARM

REGRIP

ONE ARM ON EACH SIDE OF THE POLE

USING CORE AND ARM GRIP ON TOP POLES ... BEGIN TO LIFT UP BOTOM LEG

pg 7

YOU MUST LIFT YOUR BODY OFF THE FABRIC WITH YOUR ARMS WHILE LIFTING YOUR LEG UP

DO NOT LET YOUR BODYWEIGHT REST ON THE FABRIC AT YOUR LOWER BACK

RIGHT FOOT MUST PASS BETWEEN THE POLES

YOUR RIGHT ANKLE RESTS AGAINST THE CLOSEST TOP POLE

THIS IS NOT A SECURE AND LOCKED HOLD, YOU MUST BE AWARE OF YOUR TOP FOOT AND HOLD TENSION SO THAT IT DOES NOT SLIP OFF

4. Grip the pole with both hands firmly and pull your right leg up to the top poles.
5. Feed your foot between the poles and press it against the left side of your front top pole.

tip

1. There will be alot of tension when trying to lift your right leg to the top poles. This is created becuse of the fabric pole that runs behind your back. Use both hands to pull up and lift your body slightly off that area as you lift your leg. This will ease the tension and help you raise your right leg.

2. Try to actually rest your upper ankle on the top poles when wedging your right foot in. To do this engage your right leg. Act as if the top pole is the ceiling and you are trying to push your foot through it. Lift through the hips and press down with your left base leg into the left footlock as you do this.

This is NOT a locked secure hold. Your foot can easily slip off the fabric if you are not staying engaged! DO NOT attempt alone unless you have mastered this with a coach present.

7. KIDNEY CRUSHER
IN DOUBLE FOOTLOCK

There are a few unique shapes you can take on from this pose! Two of them pictured above! The more traditional version being on the left. The next few pages describe entry and variations you can take!

SLIDE SHOULDER THROUGH

REACH LEFT ARM ACROSS BODY

1. Start in a right dominant forward facing incline split (pg 3) and crochete your right arm up around the front pole.
2. Feed your left arm and then shoulder through the poles so your back/shoulder blades rest against the fabric.
3. Grip the fabric with your left hand by reaching across the front of your chest and twisting your torso gently.

!tip

1. You MUST have staggard footlocks. One foot MUST be higher than the other. The higher the better!
2. The LOWER foot is considered the front foot for this pose.

pg 9

4. Look over your right shoulder, follow with your body and begin to lift your right leg up to the top of the poles.

7. Pass your right foot through to the other side of the poles and grip onto your ankle around the outside.
8. From there lean and pull your foot down into a split pose.

LIFT BODY AND RAISE LEG

THROUGH THE FABRIC

AROUND THE POLE AND GRAB

tip

1. Lift your body weight off the fabric during this whole entry. Otherwise there will be too much tension for you to get around.
2. Press down hard into the left leg footlock in order to lift your hips up nice and high. This will help create smooth lines and get your hips in a better alignment.

REMINDER:

This is an extremely tight wrap around your waist and can be painful. Keep your core engaged for protection throughout this pose.

7a. KIDNEY CRUSHER
VARIATIONS

1. TRADITIONAL
Ankle hold with right arm and arch your back

2. TWIST
Ankle hold with left arm, twist and arch your back

3. COMPASS
Use both hands and pull leg behind your right shoulder blade

3a. COMPASS
Same as compass but turn and look to your front foot

pg 11

8. CROSSBACK STRADDLE
FROM A DOUBLE FOOTLOCK

REMINDER:

Crossback straddles are very dangerous to learn on your own. There are many ways you can hurt yourself or get stuck. Please do not teach yourself from these pictures as a book cannot spot or save you if you get stuck in a precarious position. TO EXIT: Reach back up for the poles and stand up. Uncross the poles behind you to get back into your original DFL. Be careful as it easy to lose your grip when uncrossing poles.

BOOTY PASSES TO THE OUTSIDE OF THE RIGHT POLE

FREE AND REGRIP LEFT ARM

1. Start in DFL, place your upper body to the front of the left pole. Your right arm should be in a standard grip to the top of the pole and your left arm gripping the bottom pole.
2. Keep the pole of the fabric resting along your back, bend your right knee and twist your booty so that it slides to the outside of the right pole.
3. You want to keep rotating until your left arm can be free and grip the other pole.

ONE POLE UNDER EACH ARMPIT

4. Grip the poles of the fabric with each arm, straighten out and widen your legs so you are officially in 'X' back position.
5. Using your arms and core, lift your legs up to the sky and then invert.
6. Rotate yourself completely upside down! :)
7. Exiting can be precarious, it's best to consult with your local coach before attempting.

8a. PANCAKE
A CROSSBACK VARIATION

1. To get into pancake simply rotate back up from Crossback Straddle (pg 12) until your back is parallel to the floor.

2. Find a balance point in which your booty can hang over the fabric while your arch your back over the other side! It's a counter balance move! :)

!tip

Allow your lower back to arch and your booty to hang over the other edge of the fabric. Use your hips to act as the counterbalance weight for your upper body. .

9. CLEOPATRA
FROM CROSSBACK STRADDLE

⚠️ You MUST be aware and put the proper leg through the poles when called for. IF you do the wrong leg you will FALL out!

REMINDER:

Cleopatra is a very elegent pose but also requires alot of counterbalance awareness to keep yourself in a proper inverted split! You must find the sweet spot on your lower back as well as twist your hips slightly.

The OUTER pole and the foot it connects to is the leg you will use to put through the poles! It's very important to understand this! Reach behind you and feel which is your outer or top lying pole. Then follow it down to your foot. Whichever foot you connect to is the foot you must use!

pg 14

1. Figure out which leg you need to use FIRST before entering Crossback Straddle. (pg 12)

PULL YOUR WEIGHT OFF THE FABRIC AND BEGIN TO RAISE LEGS UP

BRING CHOSEN LEG THROUGH THE CENTER OF THE POLES

2. Rotate until your back is parallel to the floor and then bring your legs together towards the top of the fabric.

> **tip** Because your bodyweight is resting in the fabric this can be very hard. Use your arms to lift your hips and booty up off the fabric slightly.

3. Once your legs are close to the poles bring the chosen footlock through the center of the poles and pull it forward. Simultaneously send your other leg behind you and split open.

> **tip** It's best if most of this is done BEFORE you set your weight fully back down into the fabric.

4. To exit just hold the poles and lower both feet down to a stand. Back out the way you came.

10. STARFISH

FROM CROSSBACK STRADDLE

REMINDER:

This pose takes alot of body awareness and is actually pretty tricky. Seeing it demonstrated by an instructor will aid greatly. TO EXIT: simply let your hands go and you will lower back into a crossback straddle.

THUMBS DOWN - GRIP AROUND THE OUTSIDE OF YOUR LEGS AND FABRIC

YOU MUST LEAVE SPACE BETWEEN YOUR GRIP AND YOUR BOOTY.

1. **Start in a Crossback Straddle** (pg 12) **, reach up and grip each pole with each hand.**

   tip Reach as far up the fabric as possible without tilting so far that you come out. You really want to have your back parallel to the floor.

2. **Bring your legs together and keep them pointing up towards the sky.**

   tip You will have to use your grip to lift your hips up slightly off the fabric. Otherwise you will have too much tension to bring your legs together.

3. **Reach around the outside of your legs/fabric and regrip each pole with thumbs down.**

   tip Make sure to regrip just as high and DO NOT let your hand grip slide down as you go into this pose. If your hands slide down you will no longer have enough room to get your hips pushed through.

4. **Drop your head down, look to the floor while and then begin to arch your back. While doing this also push your hips through your arm grip and straddle your legs.**

11. EIFFEL TOWER
FROM A DOUBLE FOOTLOCK

tip

1. You will need lots of extra tail below your footlocks in order to complete this one.
2. Do not stand up straight after you have completed all the wraps or your wraps will fall off. Instead enter into the split from a lower squatted position.

VIEW FLIP

RIGHT HAND RIGHT TAIL

LEFT HAND LEFT TAIL

1. From a DFL, squat down with the poles between your thighs.
2. Reach your right hand down and grab your right tail. Lift it up and cross it over both knees to the other side.
3. Then reach your left hand down for your left tail and cross it over both knees to the other side.
4. End result is your tails are crossed and resting over your knees

FABRICS CROSSED OVER

pg 17

REACH BEHIND BACK AND GRAB OPPOSITE TAIL

PULL TAIL BEHIND BACK, OVER ONE THIGH AND PLACE IN BETWEEN LEGS

5. With your right hand reach BEHIND your back and grab the fabric on the opposit side.
6. Once you grab the tail pull it around your back, up over the right thigh and place the tail between your legs.

REACH BEHIND BACK

BRING TAIL AROUND BACK AND UP

DROP TAIL IN BETWEEN THIGHS

7. Repeat by reaching the left hand behind your back to grab the tail, bring it up over the left thigh place in between your legs.

8. Once both tails are in between the thighs, hold onto the poles of your fabric, keep your hips low and straighten out your legs into a split.

pg 18

12. KITE SPLIT
FROM DOUBLE FOOTLOCKS

REMINDER:

All of your weight is held up by your top arm in this pose. Be sure to practice low to make sure your grip is strong enough.

SQUAT ON DOUBLE FOOTLOCKS

LEFT HAND REACHES BEHIND POLE TO GRAB THE OTHER SIDE

GRAB TAILS WITH RIGHT HAND

EXTEND INTO SPLIT

1. Start in DFL's and squat down with both poles between your thighs.
2. Reach your left hand behind the left pole and grab the right pole.
3. Reach down with your right hand and grab both tails.
4. Extend and straighten both legs into a split.

tip

Your top hand must go behind the opposite pole with your thumb facing upwards grip. This is what creates the lock. Without this your top poles will just spread open.

pg 19

13. SINGLE PANEL SPLIT ⚠️

FROM A DFL ON ONE FABRIC POLE

REMINDER:

The trickiest part of this pose is learning the best way to wrap your foot. I've noticed some people just hold the fabric between their big toes but I prefer to have some sort of lock as a wrap!

⚠️

Be mindful of your toe grip so as not to fall.

BEGIN SFL ON EDGE OF PANEL

TRANSFER WEIGHT TO THAT SIDE

SFL ON OTHER EDGE OF SAME PANEL

PUSH OUT TO A SPLIT

1. Perform a single footlock on one pole to use as a base/support while you begin.
2. Open up the free pole, find the edge of the fabric and do a footlock on just the edge of the fabric.

tip This can be tricky. I've done my best to show a diagram of how this lock is done. It only works with a specific footlock (the figure 8 version)

3. From there step into that footlock and release the other leg.
4. Footlock the free leg onto the other edge of the same silk panel you are on.
5. Then simply push out into a split.

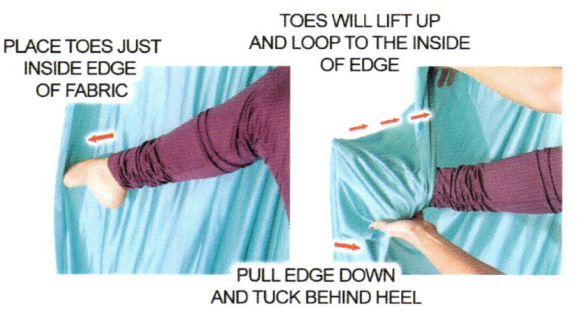

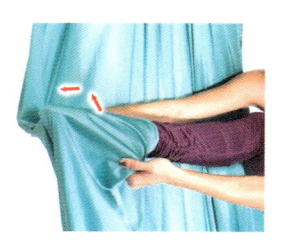

PLACE TOES JUST INSIDE EDGE OF FABRIC

TOES WILL LIFT UP AND LOOP TO THE INSIDE OF EDGE

PULL EDGE DOWN AND TUCK BEHIND HEEL

TOES SET FIRMLY INTO LOCK

pg 20

CHAPTER TWO
POSES FROM SINGLE FOOTLOCKS

Welcome to Chapter Two! This section includes a list of all my favorite poses that stem from Single Footlocks! Remember to use this book as a guide and never by itself. You should always have a competent instructor present.

Below is a quick image reference of the main poses covered in this section (variations not pictured).

pg 23

pg 23

pg 24

pg 25

pg 26

pg 27

pg 28

pg 29

pg 30

pg 31

continued on next page . . .

pg 21

. . . continuation

pg 34

pg 35

pg 36

pg 38

pg 39

pg 41

pg 42

pg 43

pg 44

pg 46

14. LEAN OUT SPLIT
WITH AN ELBOW GRIP

1. Starting in a right footlock, wrap your right elbow around the fabric.
2. Grab your left ankle with your left hand.
3. Lean out and extend your left leg.

15. LEAN OUT SPLIT
WITH A HAND GRIP

1. Starting in a right wrap your right elbow around the fabric.
2. Grab your left ankle with your left hand.
3. Lean out and extend your left leg.

The grips can be surprisingly difficult and you could peel off. Please practice this low until you can hold easily for 8-10 seconds!

16. DANCER SPLIT

FROM A SINGLE FOOTLOCK

FEED RIGHT ARM THROUGH

TWIST UNTIL BACK IS AGAINST FABRIC

REGRIP LEFT ARM OVER FABRIC

1. With your right foot locked, grab the fabric with your left hand above your head.
2. Feed your right arm and shoulder between your body and the fabric.
3. Continue twisting through until your back is against the fabric.
4. Reposition your grip so the pole of the fabric is resting in your left armpit.

tip Using a crochete wrap (not pictured) with your arm is an even smoother process for entering. Consult your local teacher for tips on using a crochete method.

PUSH HIP OUT TO THE SIDE

KEEP POLE IN ARMPIT

5. Push your booty and your free leg away (to the left) from the fabric.

tip You MUST keep the pole of the fabric in your left armpit during all of this!

6. Release your left arm, bend your left knee and grab your left ankle.
7. Other arm can hold onto the fabric or release for balance.

tip In order to balance you need to sink your weight deep down to the floor.

I have seen aerialists lose grip or fall off balance easily while entering and exiting this pose. Please be cautious and practice low.

17. LAYBACK SPLIT
FROM A SINGLE FOOTLOCK

REMINDER:

Alot of weight bears down on your hip and in your hand grip on the pole. As always test this low and be sure your hips are properly conditioned. Consult your local teacher for best ways to prepare your hips and grip strength.

1. Split the poles and bring your hips into the center, DO NOT bring your arm through the poles
2. Keep the pole of the fabric in your armpit, bring your free leg up in a bent knee position and grab your heel.

FABRIC IS UNDER YOUR ARMPIT AND OVER YOUR HIP/THIGH CREASE

FABRIC IN HIP CREASE - YOUR PIVOT POINT

3. Hold the fabric low with your other hand and begin to straighten out your free leg.
4. Begin to lean back while simultaneously setting the fabric deep into your hip crease.
5. Bodyweight should be distributed between your right hand holding the fabric and your hip crease resting on the fabric.

tip

1. The fabric must fall into your hip crease, think of this is the pivot point, you will not be able to fully lean back until you have set your weight onto this pivot point.
2. Press firmly into your base footlock and keep that leg strong and straight.
3. You will bear your weight evenly between your pivot point hip crease AND your other hand grip holding the pole of the fabric. DO NOT put all of your weight onto just the hip crease point.

pg 25

18. SIDE SPLIT
FROM A SINGLE FOOTLOCK

ROTATE UNTIL BACK IS FACING FABRIC

1. In a RSFL, look to your left side, twist your body to the left and rotate 180 degrees so that your back/booty is against the fabric.

2. Then regrip so that your left arm/armpit is placed against the pole of the fabric.

3. Grip pole above your head with BOTH hands.
4. Slide hips over so the pole of fabric is resting against your back.
5. Using core and arms lift your free leg up to the top of the pole and place the sole of your foot against the fabric!

REPOSITION GRIP

SLIDE HIPS OVER SO FABRIC IS AT YOUR LOWER BACK

tip: Lift both legs up as you begin to enter the pose. Think of it as a straddle lift where both legs are coming up initially! This helps especially if you do not have alot of flexibility in your middle splits!

This is not a secure lock! Your are merely using the sole of your foot as grip against the fabric. Practice mindfully and with caution so that your foot does not slip off the pole of the fabric.

19. SPLIT TILT
FROM A SIDE SPLIT

Please be cautious entering and exiting this pose. If you lose both hand points of contact while entering/exiting you will fall.

PRESS INTO POLE TO HELP INVERT

GRIP FOOT AND SET BACK DOWN

1. Starting from a side split (pg26) reach up and grip the pole of the fabric with both hands.
2. Pull into an inverted straddle position.
3. Once inverted, release your left hand and grab your left ankle.
4. Once the ankle is gripped set your right leg back down and release your right hand.

tip

Be sure to keep the pole of the fabric running along your lower back for the whole duration of this pose. During Step 2 it will help greatly to lift your body weight out of the fabric. Treat the lift as if you were truly about to invert, which would help to lift your bodyweight off the fabric.

pg 27

20. BIRD OF PARADISE
FROM A SIDE SPLIT

INVERT FROM SIDE SPLIT

REACH AROUND THIGH

MEET HANDS TOGETHER

EXTEND SPLIT

1. Begin from an entry into split tilt (pg 27) Instead of grabbing your ankle reach your arm over your knee pit and bend the knee. The back of your hand should rest near the top of your bottom.
2. Settle into this position with your top knee bent and then begin to bend your lower arm behind your back so that both hands meet together.
3. Once you have firmly gripped your hands together you can straighten out your top leg.

Please be cautious entering and exiting this pose. If you lose both hand points of contact while entering/exiting you will fall.
This pose requires an extreme amount of shoulder flexibility. Practice the standing 'Bird of Paradise' yoga pose on the floor first.

21. COMPASS POSE
FROM A SIDE SPLIT

REMINDER:

The fabric poles absolutely must be running along the inside of both thighs.
TO EXIT: Do not stand up, stay in a squatted position as your release your top leg and regrip the poles with your hands.

FABRIC ALONG THE INSIDE OF THE BENT KNEE

1. Starting from a side split (pg 26) bend your top knee over the fabric.
2. Regrip so your are holding the pole of the fabric above your knee.
3. Bend your bottom knee and allow your body to slide down the fabric. You MUST keep the poles running along the inside of both thighs.
4. Push against the fabric with one hand and straighten your top leg with the other.

VIEW FLIP

PULL WITH ONE HAND

PUSH WITH ONE HAND

tip During Step 4: Having one hand on the fabric and the other pulling on the leg will help you to hold tension and not fall out of the pose.

pg 29

22. SPATCHCOCK ⚠️
FROM A SINGLE FOOTLOCK

REMINDER:

TO EXIT: Get your head/shoulders free first before removing the top leg.

⚠️

Be aware of your top foot grip as well as your shoulder grip pressing against the poles. Both of these are not secure holds and have poential for you to slip out.

SHIFT HIPS OVER SO LOWER BACK IS OVER FABRIC

LIFT LEG AND PRESS FOOT AGAINST THE FABRIC

PLACE BACK OF NECK AGAINST THE POLE BUT DO NOT LET POLE SLIP OFF SHOULDERS

1. From a single foolock, split the poles and bring your free leg through. DO NOT bring your arms through – leave the poles resting in your armpits.
2. Slide your booty to the side so the pole of the fabric is resting against your lower back.
3. Lift your free leg up to the top of the pole, press the sole of your foot against the fabric.
4. Pull your head to the other pole and bring it to the front so the fabric is resting on the back of your neck. DO NOT let the fabric slip off the neck.
5. Straighten your arms along the fabric to create tension and balance.

pg 30

23. MERMAID SPLIT
FROM A SINGLE FOOTLOCK

SPLIT POLES BRING FREE LEG THROUGH AND TURN TO THE RIGHT

CHEST RESTS AGAINST RIGHT POLE

BODY BEGINS TO LEAN OUT TO THE LEFT AWAY FROM THE FABRIC

1. From a RSFL split the poles, bring your left leg through and turn towards the right pole so that your chest and front of your hips are resting against the right pole.

> **tip:** Both hands are on the right pole and this becomes your focus, you will be rotating your body in circles around this pole.

2. Lean your body out to the left away from the fabric and then begin to turn your body to face the fabric.

3. After leaning out turn your body back to face the fabric.
4. Raise your free leg OVER the pole closest to you, press it against the other pole.

> **tip** Your free leg must go OVER the pole thats currently the "left pole" once you have turned to face the fabric.

TURN BACK TO FACE THE FABRIC

LEFT LEG PASSES OVER LEFT POLE AND PRESSES AGAINST RIGHT POLE

PUSH BODY BACK UP AND INTO THE FABRIC

BEGIN TO ROTATE AROUND AGAIN

5. Once your foot has pressed against the the other pole you must push it with slight force so that that piece of fabric moves down of your calf muscle to your ankle.

> **tip** Typically when rotating around the fabric it will get caught on the calf muscle so you must push it down to the ankle.

6. Then continue your whole body rotation by bring your body back up into the fabric and setting your hips and chest against the pole once more.

7. Complete this process 1-2 more times depending on your comfort level. The more times you roll the more intense of a stretch you will feel.

> **tip** Typically on the 3rd time around you won't need to use your foot to press the other pole down.

8. Reach down with your left arm and grab your left foot.
9. Extend into split! :)

REMINDER:

TO EXIT: Hold the pole above your head with both hands and reverse the roll. Go back the way you came. Do so slowly as momentum can pull you off balance.

24. FROG SPLIT
FROM A SINGLE MERMAID WRAP

REMINDER:

Also this pose can be very tight and strenuous on your knee so please get into it with caution and come out if it is not bearable! TO EXIT: Pull back up to a stand and roll out the way you came in.

tip

This middle split comes from a single mermaid wrap. It's important to note that you DO NOT push the fabric down to the ankle as you do in the traditional mermaid wrap.

1. Complete one Mermaid Roll Up (pg 31) WITHOUT using your foot to push the fabric down to the calf muscles. For this pose you want to have the fabric riding high up your thigh.

FALL OUT TO THE LEFT AND TWIST TOWARDS THE FABRIC

LEG GOES UP AND THROUGH WITHOUT PUSHING THE POLE DOWN TO THE ANKLE

2. Once back in your original position, fall out of the fabric to the left, bend your right knee and sink down into the lock created by the fabric.

DROP DOWN TO THE PIT OF YOUR KNEE

EXTEND INTO SPLIT

3. Get a firm grip with your right hand, grab your free foot with your left and extend into a middle split.

pg 34

25. COMPASS KNEE HANG

FROM MERMAID WRAP

REMINDER:

This one can cause alot of stress to your knee so please proceed with caution!
TO EXIT: Grab the poles and pull all the way up to a stand. Reverse roll out the direction you rolled in from.

1. Once in Frog Split (pg34) let go and hang upside down, bring your free leg to the front of your body and then begin to wedge it behind your shoulder.
2. If your left leg is your free leg then you will be wedging it behind your left shoulder. Use your right hand to grip your left foot to keep it wedged behind you.

Keep your knee bent and engaged.

pg 35

26. REVERSE MERMAID SPLIT

FROM REVERSE MERMAID WRAP

tip: A Reverse Mermaid Wrap is required for this pose and has a similar start to the traditional Mermaid Roll Up. In fact you complete one full Mermaid Roll Up rotation before things begin to change!

1. Complete one full rotation of a traditional Mermaid Roll Up (pg 31)

LEAN OUT

TURN TO FACE FABRIC

BRING KNEE TO FABRIC BUT NOT OVER IT

KNEE AND LEG GOES UNDER THE POLE OF THE FABRIC

2. Then you are going to do HALF a Mermaid Roll Up, lean out and turn back to the fabric placing your knee to the pole.
3. DO NOT put your leg over the fabric. Your leg/knee is going to go UNDER the pole of the fabric you are holding onto.

BEND ELBOW AND ARM OVER FABRIC

KEEP TURNING IN UNTIL YOU CAN REST YOUR BACK COMFORTABLY IN THE FABRIC

4. Once your leg passes under the pole bring your left arm/elbow up and over that same pole.
5. Begin to rotate your body and turn in so that your back comes into the fabric.

> **tip** You should be able to rest your back and body comfortably enough to where you could even let go with one hand. Fabric should be on your lower back.

FABRIC STAYS AT LOWER BACK

INVERT AND STRADDLE

GRAB YOUR ANKLE AND PULL INTO A SPLIT

6. Once settled in, reach back up and grab each pole with each hand.
7. Lift your free leg up and invert back over.

> **tip** The fabric MUST still be resting along your lower back. If its too low you will feel like you are going to slip out.

8. After you invert, grab your free leg and straighten it out into a split.

REMINDER:
There is alot of directional changes when getting into and out of this pose. Practice with an experienced instructor so as not to get tangled/twisted.

27. FLOATING GENIE
FROM REVERSE MERMAID WRAP

REMINDER:

This pose stems from a Reverse Mermaid Wrap (pg 36) You should practice and be comfortable with Reverse Mermaid first before attempting to do this pose.

1. Reach up from Reverse Mermaid Wrap and place the left pole against the left armpit.

> **tip** Fabric should be resting along your lower back. Booty should not be sitting in the fabric.

2. From there grab your left ankle with the left hand and extend into a middle split.

pg 38

28. NEEDLE SPLIT
FROM A SINGLE FOOTLOCK

REMINDER:

There's a decent amount of steps to go through to get into Needle Split as well as some fall potential. Always practice with a trained instructor present. TO EXIT: Be sure to get a firm grip with both hands back on the poles before releasing top leg.

HOLD RIGHT POLE AND LEAN AWAY

TWIST THROUGH THE FABRIC SO THE RIGHT SHOULDER AND BACK GO THROUGH THE FABRIC FIRST

1. Based off of a right footlock, hold onto the right side pole and lean back away from the fabric.
2. Pull your right arm/elbow back in towards the fabric and hook your right elbow of the right pole you are holding on to. While you are doing this you are also turning your back into the fabric so that your back begins to go through the poles.

!tip

The direction for which to rotate can be a little confusing. Essentially you are bringing your right side everything into the center of the poles and twisting so that your back goes through the center of the poles.

pg 39

3. Continue with the motion of your back going through the fabric until your whole body and leg are completely through.

4. Once your whole body and leg comes through, grab the other pole with your left hand and stand your body upright.

5. You MUST CROSS THE FABRIC once and then bring your top half through the poles and into a forward fold position.

CROSS THE FABRIC BEFORE COMING THROUGH INTO A FORWARD FOLD

⚠️ Between stages 4-5 you will have to cross the fabric. Not doing so could result in not enough tension and cause you to fall out of the pose.

CROCHETE FROM THE OUTSIDE IN

6. Once you fold, regrip the fabric with your thumbs pointing up.
7. Lift your free leg up to the top of the pole and wrap your leg FROM THE OUTSIDE IN.

pg 40

29. STARGAZER SPLIT
FROM A SINGLE FOOTLOCK

tip

The more you can arch your back and slide your shoulders low down on the fabric the more vertical and extreme this split will look!

HIPS / LEFT LEG ONLY THROUGH THE FABRIC AND OFF TO THE LEFT SIDE

BRING YOUR LEFT LEG UP AND BEND KNEE OVER INTO THE FABRIC

1. From an RSFL, split the poles, bring your waist and left leg through the poles and off to the left side (so that the pole is resting against your lower back). DO NOT bring your arms through, only your left leg and hips
2. Invert slightly and bring your left leg up to the top of the pole.
3. Hook your left leg by bending your left knee over the pole and resting it into position.

pg 41

PULL RIGHT SHOULDER INTO FABRIC POLE

ONCE SETTLED IN STRAIGHTEN TOP LEG

4. Once your left knee is hooked pull your right shoulder into the fabric.
5. Square your hips forward and settle the shoulders as low down on the fabric.
6. Straighten your top leg into a split!

30. ATHENA SPLIT
FROM A SINGLE FOOTLOCK

Even though this split is very similar in looks to Stargazer, I wanted to give its own name instead of just calling it a variation. The reason is because achieving this straight arm position takes a profound amount of strength and balance. It is challenging and being able to do Stargazer does not mean you will be able to do Athena.

> tip: This split is much easier to perform on stretchy fabric versus low stretch!

1. To achieve this start out in Stargazer, (pg 41) grab the pole of the fabric just above your head and begin to straighten both your arms and your leg!

31. BOW AND ARROW
FROM A SINGLE FOOTLOCK

REMINDER:

Bow and Arrow hits you most intensely in your hip flexors during the entry and exit! Be sure to warm up your hip flexors alot before attempting this one!

SLIDE HIPS TO THE SIDE

INVERT AND LIFT

WRAP TOES AROUND FABRIC

1. Start out like Stargazer (pg 29) except crochete your entire leg around the top pole.

   tip It's imperative that your press the sole of your foot against the fabric and kep the tension throughout the entire entry.

2. Press your toes into the fabric, bend your left knee, lift your body up and begin to twist into the center of the poles. This can be extremely intense on your hip flexors!

KNEE BENDS AND PUSHES INWARD

PULL BODYWEIGHT UP

KEEP TOES HOOKED AROUND FABRIC

tip

The secret for working with tight hip flexors here is to lift your body weight out of the fabric as much as possible while turning in and then set your body down into the pose once completely turned in!

pg 43

32. RUSSIAN SPLIT ⚠️
FROM A SINGLE FOOTLOCK

⚠️ This is a very dangerous split move and extremely stressful to the hamstrings! Release down slowly into this split as it is possible for you to either over rotate or for the fabric to slip off your shoulders! Be very mindful or your speed, split control and if the fabric feels secure against your shoulders. DO NOT practice this if you are a beginner! Practice only with the go ahead from your aerial instructor!

START IN RSFL AND SPLIT POLES

FABRIC MUST CATCH UNDER ARMPIT

LEFT LEG AND WHOLE BUM GOES THROUGH THE SPLIT POLES

LIFT AND HOOK LEFT LEG AND FOOT

KEEP FABRIC ALONG LOWER BACK

MOVE YOUR LEFT HAND OVER TO THE RIGHT POLE

1. In an RSFL, split the poles and bring your left leg through the fabric. Continue going until your bum is all the way through and your lower back is resting against the pole.

   (tip) DO NOT bring your left arm through. The fabric should catch and stay under your left armpit.

2. Keep your lower back against the fabric, lift your free leg up into the air and set the inner sole of your foot against the pole.

   (tip) Remember to keep the fabric at your lower back. If it slides down and off your bum you could fall out.

3. Switch your hands so your left hand is holding the opposite pole. What was the right pole. The pole your top foot is NOT on.

FEED RIGHT ARM THROUGH POLES

FEED ARM THROUGH UNTIL THE POLE SITS AGAINST THE BACK OF YOUR SHOULDER. REPEAT WITH THE OTHER ARM.

STRAIGHTEN ARMS UP THE POLES AND REGRIP

BE SURE THE FABRIC IS SET FIRMLY BEHIND THE SHOULDERS

4. Once left hand is holding right side pole, feed your right arm down to the floor and through the fabric at your base foot.

> **tip** You are basically doing a forward fold motion and bringing your arm/shoulder through so that the fabric pole near your foot is resting against the back of your shoulder/neck.

5. Repeat the same motion with the other arm.

> **tip** Keep your top foot hooked around the fabric to help with your stability.

6. Reach both arms up high and grab the fabric near your hips/bum. Thumbs should be facing up.
7. You must position the fabric carefully now. It should be running behind your shoulder blades. Bend your elbows slightly over the fabric.

> **tip** It feels slightly like you are squeezing the pole between your arm and body.

8. Gently release your top leg and gain your bearings.

9. If feeling secure slowly lower your back leg down.

SLOWLY RELEASE

STRAIGHTEN AND LOWER YOUR BACK LEG

ROTATE SLOWLY AND CAREFULLY SO AS NOT TO GO TOO FAR

BE MINDFUL THE FABRIC DOES NOT SLIP OFF THE SHOULDERS

10. Tilt carefully so that you do not over rotate!

33. INVERSE SPLIT
FROM A RUSSIAN SPLIT

REMINDER:

I show how this move comes after a russian split pose. Consult with your local instructor for other entries!

⚠️ Weak grip or over-rotating can cause you to fall. Lower into this SLOWLY. As always these moves are best to be practiced with an instructor and in a safe place!

RAISE FOOT UP TO POLE AND BRACE AGAINST FABRIC FIRST

GENTLY PASS SHOULDERS THROUGH THE FABRIC

RELEASE LEG AND LOWER DOWN INTO A SPLIT

1. From a Russian Split (pg 44) bring your leg back up to the pole and brace your foot against it.

   💡 *tip* You can hook, crochet or just rest your foot against the pole.

2. Slide your shoulders one at a time between the fabric so that they release and point down towards the ground.

3. Release your top leg from the poles and bring it back down into a split. Remember to lower slowly so as not to over rotate.

CHAPTER THREE

- POSES WITH A SFL + FREE POLE
- POSES FROM WRIST WRAPS

Welcome to Chapter Three! Here I cover poses that use single footlocks on only one pole while the other pole is free flowing. I also touch on a few poses involving wrist wraps! Below is your quick reference guide to the poses covered.

pg 48

pg 49

pg 50

pg 51

pg 53

pg 55

pg 56

pg 58

pg 60

pg 61

pg 62

pg 63

34. FLAG SPLIT
SFL ON SPLIT POLES

tip

Flag split requires a great amount of arm strength. However, crocheting both arms around the fabric will greatly increase your ability to hold on! I also recommend crocheting the top arm first before the bottom arm. Not necessary but has always been a better process for me!

1. RSFL on split poles, reach your right arm high and crochete it around the free pole. The free pole should end up resting behind your back.
2. Keep the free pole running along your back and crochete your left arm down along the bottom of the free pole.

3. Get a solid grip with both hands and begin to lean out to the left, bring your free foot up into your left hand and extend into a split!

FABRIC MOVES BEHIND BACK

CROCHETE BOTH ARMS

BRING FREE FOOT TO FREE HAND

EXTEND OUT

pg 48

35. TWISTED FLAG SPLIT
SFL ON SPLIT POLES

1. RSFL on split poles, reach your LEFT arm high and crochet it around the free pole.
2. Make sure the free pole is running behind your back and then crochete your right arm down on the bottom of the free pole.
3. Leading with your right hand, turn completely to your left so that you pass under the other pole and push out to the side.

BOTTOM RIGHT ARM GOES BETWEEN YOU AND THE POLE OF THE FABRIC TO THE LEFT

tip Think about feeding your right arm across your body between you and the other pole of the fabric.

GRAB FREE FOOT WITH BOTTOM ARM

4. Once here lift your free leg up and and into your base hand.
5. Get a good grip on your foot and then extend out into a split.

pg 49

36. CROSSBOW
SFL ON SPLIT POLES

💬tip This one can be done without wrapping your dominant hand, however, the wrap makes it significantly easier to hold! Be sure to drive your hips up aswell to help achieve a nice straight "arrow" line! :)

OPPOSITE ARM TO LEG

STRAIGHTEN OUT AND LIFT LEG

MAKE SURE LEG GOES AROUND TO THE OUTSIDE OF YOUR WRAPPED ARM

1. RSFL on split poles, wrap your LEFT arm in the free pole.

💬tip It makes a HUGE DIFFERENCE if you start this pose from a squatted position!

2. Once wrapped straighten your body out, lift your hips and free leg up towards the ceiling.
3. Bring your left leg to the OUTSIDE of your left arm.
4. Reach across your body with your RIGHT hand and grab your LEFT foot.
5. Pull down on and straighten your left leg as well as drive your hips up to the ceiling.

37. SPLIT BETWEEN POLES

FROM A SFL ON SPLIT POLES

The key thing for this pose is to make sure the pole of the fabric does not slip off of your hip/thigh.

RIGHT SHOULDER FEEDS THROUGH

TWIST THROUGH UNTIL YOUR BACK IS AGAINST THE FABRIC

REGRIP SO ONE ARM IS AROUND EACH POLE

1. Start in a RSFL on one pole. For now don't pay much attention to the other pole. Your main focus is working around the pole you are footlocked onto.

2. With your left arm grab the pole of the fabric above your head and begin to slide your right arm/shoulder through beside and around pole.

3. Keep twisting until your back is resting against the fabric.

4. Regrip the fabric so one arm is on either side of the pole.

pg 51

5. Once your back is against the pole you can choose to hold both hands on the same pole or split your grip between the two poles.
6. Make sure your hips/left leg are scooted off to the left side.
7. Lift and press the sole of your left foot against the fabric.

!tip Some people prefer to crochete their leg however I feel its too restricting.

8. Once your foot is pressed against the pole, grab both hands onto the free pole.
9. Continue to press the sole of your foot into the fabric, bend your knee and twist your hips through so your chest is square to your free pole.

!tip Lifting your bodyweight up out of the fabric will help with this motion.

10. Once turned through allow yourself to sink back into the split.

38. MARIONETTE SPLIT
FROM A SFL ON SPLIT POLES

REMINDER:

This wrap has alot of steps and is extremely easy to get tangled up in. Especially when exiting. Please have your instructor walk you through the ins and outs of this pose before ever attempting on your own.

FREE POLE IN LEFT ARMPIT AND BEHIND BACK

WRAP FABRIC COMPLETELY AROUND YOUR BODY

LET FABRIC REST OVER RAISED LEFT LEG

1. From a RSFL on split poles. Put the free pole under your left armpit and keep it tucked in there.
2. With your right arm reach behind your back, grab the free pole and bring it all the way around your body to the front side.
3. Continue wrapping the free pole across the front of your body.

(tip) Hold your left knee high and let the fabric hook over the knee to avoid having the fabric unravel.

pg 53

BUNCH FABRIC TOGETHER AT WAIST

4. Repeat this wrap one more time around your body. There are variations and poses that only call for one wrap around the body. However I prefer two wraps for this pose.
5. Gather the fabric together around your waist, lean back and hook your left leg up over the left side pole.

🛈 tip Your left leg wraps only over the left side pole so that your leg is going in between the poles.

HOOK LEG FROM THE OUTSIDE IN TO BETWEEN THE POLES

TOP LEG TURNS UP AND OUT

BOTTOM LEG PUSHES DOWN

6. Hold onto the right side pole and pull your body upright. As you do this push your right foot down to the floor to begin to stand upright.

8. Simultaneously push your top leg out to the side and roll your hips through until your chest is square to the other pole.

🛈 tip

Lifting your body weight up out of the fabric will help with this!

END WTH KNEE AND HIP ROTATING DOWN

pg 54

39. FALLING SPLIT
FROM A MARIONETTE

REMINDER:

This pose stems from the marionette wrap. TO EXIT: Just release your split and pull back up to a stand. Pull your free leg back through the poles and let the fabric unravel.

FALL OUT AWAY FROM THE FABRIC

LOOKING OVER RIGHT SHOULDER

RIGHT LEG PUSHES BACK AWAY FROM THE BODY

1. From a Marionette Split (previous page) lean out of and away from the fabric.
2. As you lean out your locked foot kicks up and away from your body.
3. From here get a firm grip with your right hand, grab your left foot with your left hand and extend into a split.

GRAB ANKLE AND SPLIT OUT

pg 55

40. FAIRY ROLL UP SPLIT
FROM A TWISTED FLAG ENTRY

REMINDER:

This pose comes from a Fairy Roll Up wrap. To avoid a common issue of shoulder discomfort during this pose, wrap your top arm up as high on the fabric as possible! TO EXIT: Regrip pole with bottom arm, release bottom leg and reverse roll out the way you came.

tip

To complete the split you will need to pull out alot of extra slack on your initial roll through. See the last image of the diagram below. Reach your arm as far forward as you can to pull extra slack through.

LEFT ARM CROCHETE

RIGHT FOOT LOCKED

FABRIC RUNS BEHIND BACK AND CROCHETE BOTTOM ARM

TWIST UNDER AND THROUGH LOCKED POLE

REACH ARM FAR FORWARD TO CREATE EXTRA SLACK

1. RSFL on one pole and crochete your LEFT arm up HIGH on the other free fabric pole.
2. Bring the free pole behind your back and crochete your bottom arm.
3. Lead with your bottom arm, twist your body under and through the locked pole (the pole your footlock is on)
4. Twist all the way so that you are now leaning out away from the fabric with your locked foot slightly behind you.

CONTINUE TO ROTATE ALL THE WAY THROUGH

BACK TO THE ORIGINAL LEAN OUT POSITION

COMPLETE 2 OR 3 ROLL THROUGHS ENDING IN THIS POSITION

TURN BACK INTO THE FABRIC

5. Repeat this roll through again, lead with your arm and turn back in towards your locked foot.
6. Continue to roll through the fabric again.
7. Your ending position should look somewhat like the photo above on the far right. Your back leg wrapping in an arabesque, left arm high and right arm stretching out away from you.

!tip

You can chose to stop on either the 2nd or 3rd roll however I notice most like to perform 3 roll throughs.

8. From there pick up your free leg and place it into the fabric you have been holding with your bottom arm.
9. Push your leg firmly into the fabric and extend into a split.

41. UNICORN SPLIT

FROM A MARIONETTE ENTRY WRAP

REMINDER:

There are alot of steps for this one, exiting is essentially a reversal of all these steps BUT can get very confusing. Having a spotter present in case you get tangled is a good idea.

Panel labels (left to right):
- MOVE FREE TAIL OUT OF THE WAY / RSFL ON RIGHT POLE
- FREE TAIL IS AGAINST LEFT ARMPIT AND RUNNING BEHIND BACK / LEAN OVER TO THE RIGHT USING LEFT THIGH AS PIVOT POINT
- REACH BEHIND YOU WITH RIGHT HAND AND GRAB FREE TAIL
- BRING FREE TAIL ACROSS YOUR FRONT AND REST OVER LEFT THIGH
- PUSH FREE TAIL FROM ARMPIT DOWN TO HIPS

1. Start in a RSFL (entry similar to Marionette Split pg 53)
2. Place the free tail in your left armpit and then regrip the pole with your left hand.
3. Bend and lift your left knee, place the pole into the hip crease and pivot over this point.
4. Reach your right hand behind your back and grab the free tail.

tip Essentially you want the tail running under your left armpit, behind your back and then across the front of your body.

5. Stand up, bring the free tail up and cross it in front of the body letting it rest over your raised left leg.

tip Lifting/bending the left knee will stop the fabric from falling down once you cross it across your body.

6. Gently take the free tail under your armpit and push it down so it sits lower to your waist. If the fabric is too high under your armpit you will meet resistance.

7. Hold onto your free tail. Hold the tail by your left hip bone and DO NOT let go at the moment. You WILL fall out if you let go of your tail in these beginning steps.
8. Lean back, lift your free leg up and place it BETWEEN the two top fabric poles.
9. Bring your free leg through the poles. At the same time rotate your body to the right and upside down.

tip DO NOT let your legs lift up to the sky. PULL your legs down to the ground and together. As if you were doing a forward fold.

10. As you rotate, the free tail you were holding at your hip gets passed behind your back and to the other side. You should end up holding your free tail on the same side as your free leg.
11. Once there, take the free tail and wrap it between your legs and down around the free leg. All the way down until it sits against the sole of your foot. Typically this is 3-4 times.
12. Grab each tail seperately in each hand.

tip Put the tail up between the legs first to start your wrap. Hook the tail around the sole of your foot.

13. Hold the tails fairly close to your feet. Start with a very close grip and allow it to slide out as needed.
14. Keep as much pressure on the tails as possible.

tip Do not let your footlocked leg point up to the sky. Keep it as low to the ground as possible.

15. Continue holding the tails, point your free leg out to the side and begin to rotate your leg around until it is behind you in a split. Again it's important to keep your rotating leg low or parallel to the floor.
16. Once there, bring the tails together, pull on your tails to increase your split and arch your back.

42. TRIANGLE SHAPE SPLIT ⚠

FROM AN INVERTED CROCHETE WRAP & SFL

tip: Be sure to let the top knee pass over the fabric when doing your initial side hook and when rotating your body inward to complete the split. If your leg doesn't get the proper crochete you will be much more susceptible to falling out.

1. RSFL on one pole.
2. Turn in towards your right leg and pass your left leg over the pole of the fabric and to the other side.
3. Slide your hips through so that your booty is also resting on the other side.

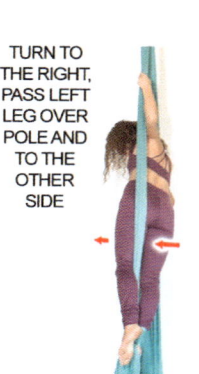

⚠ **DO NOT bring your left arm over the fabric. Your left arm must stay so that the pole is resting in your left armpit.**

4. Grip high on the poles and lift your free leg up.
5. Hook your toes against the pole of the locked fabric. You MUST hook your toes AND your knee slightly over the pole.
5. Bring your tails together, rotate your body and hips inward so that your top knee rotates around the fabric and you are in a full front split.
6. Adjust your tails so they meet down at the bottom to create the other corner of the triangle shape base.

43. INVERTED SPLIT
FROM A DOUBLE WRIST WRAP

tip

You can do this by wrapping the fabric around your wrist 2-3 times IF you are standing on the floor. If you are doing this from a climb then just a hand hang without wrapping your wrists works best.

REMINDER:

While the description to this pose may seem simple, this can be very challenging to a beginner or someone who has not yet developed the proper strength/technique. Your coach can aid greatly in providing tools/tips to help build the form needed for this!

1. Grip the each pole with each hand.
2. Pull up with your arms/core and bring your feet up to the ceiling.
3. Once your legs have lifted slightly over halfway, allow your head/shoulders to drop to the floor.
4. Once upside down and balanced slowly split your legs.

.

Remember when exiting to always lower your booty to the floor. DO NOT do a complete flip through the fabric unless you are experienced in that manuever. You can damage your shoulders very easily!

pg 61

43a. INVERTED STAG
VARIATION FROM A DOUBLE WRIST WRAP

1. From an inverted split (previous page 62) bend both knees at a 90 or 120 degree angle to achieve the stag variation.

44. SPLIT THROUGH BIRDS NEST
FROM DOUBLE WRIST WRAP

1. Wrist wrap invert with your legs together, set the top (front) of your left ankle against the pole of the fabric.

   tip Do not WRAP your ankle. Your are simply pressing the top of the ankle against the fabric and using your toes as slight grip. This can be very confusing in the beginning.

2. Point your right foot down to the floor. Let your hips/leg slide down towards the floor.
3. Arch your back and look up to the sky.

REMINDER: TO EXIT: Press the top foot hard against the fabric, tuck your nose into your belly and drive your booty back up to the center of the poles.

PLEASE practice this low to the floor. It is possible to slide to far/arch so much that you cannot pull yourself out back out. This will force you to slip your foot off and potentially injur your shoulders.

45. ALIEN SPLIT
FROM DOUBLE WRIST WRAP

REMINDER:

This pose is extremely strenuous on your shoulders/hips/grip and hammies! Only advanced aerialists should attempt this. This pose requires BOTH strength and flexibility.

LEFT LEG COMES THROUGH POLES

FROG RIGHT LEG TO OUTSIDE OF POLE

WEDGE SHOULDER DEEP UNDER THIGH

1. Grip each pole with each hand then begin to invert.
2. Split open your legs as you invert and allow ONLY your left leg to go through the poles.
3. During this process frog your right leg and keep it to the outside of the pole.
4. As you continue to bring your hips through, wedge your right shoulder under the leg your frogged out.

tip This "wedge" is key to having a good alien split. It will be your focal balance point. Practice on the floor by doing a low lunge and wedge your shoulder as deep under your front lunging leg as you can.

5. Once you feel you have a good wedge straighten out your legs. You should still be at an angle and not fully lowered when you straighten your legs.
6. Once the legs are set pass your hips deeper through the poles and begin to level out your split.

HIPS PASS THROUGH POLES AFTER WEDGE IS SET AND LEGS ARE STRAIGHT

CHAPTER FOUR
POSES WITH AN INVERT ENTRY

Welcome to Chapter Four, here you will find poses that stem from a full body inversion. The inversions may vary in detail, such as double leg crochete versus single leg crochete as well as inverts using knee hooks. A thorough understanding of crochete and knee hook motions is detrimental to your success. Many of these poses require great body awareness, knowledge of fabric theory and strength. Do not take aerial lightly. Pictures make poses look simple, respect the arts and your safety. Some of these poses are and can be extremely dangerous to a novice.

pg 66

pg 68

pg 70

pg 71

pg 72

pg 73

pg 74

pg 77

pg 79

pg 64

pg 81
pg 82
pg 83
pg 84
pg 86
pg 88
pg 90
pg 91
pg 92
pg 93
pg 94
pg 96
pg 98
pg 99
pg 100

pg 65

46. STELLAR SPLIT
FROM AN INVERTED CROCHETE WRAP

REMINDER:

Hip flexor flexibility is greatly needed to rotate up into the pose. There are other entries that require less focus on hip flexor rotation, so if this entry is a challenge try hiring your instructor for a private tutorial of another entry! :)

SPLIT POLES

INVERT

CROCHETE LEG AND TOES

RELEASE OPPOSITE ARM

REACH BEHIND BACK FOR SAME SIDE TAIL

1. Split the poles and invert, crochete the right leg around the same side pole.
2. Release your left arm, reach behind your back and the working tail. The same tail your right leg is crocheted on.

TAIL TO THE INSIDE OF THIGH

FEED TAIL UP OVER AND BETWEEN LEGS

REPEAT WRAPS ALL THE WAY DOWN YOUR LEG

HOOK TAIL ON SOLE OF FOOT

3. Bring the working tail to the INSIDE of thigh and then hook over and around leg.

> tip The direction of wrap is front to back. Wrap from the inside of thigh over to the outside.

4. Repeat this circular wrapping all the way down your leg and hook over the sole of your foot.

JOIN FABRIC TOGETHER

WALK HANDS AND CHEST UP THE POLE

TWIST HIPS FRONT KNEE FACING DOWN

PUSH TAILS OUT

5. Reach for free tail and join both tails together in your hands.
6. Begin to twist your hips so that they are square to the floor. Front leg knee should be facing down.

> tip Keep your toes crocheted around the fabric and to help your rotation, try bending your top leg knee and lifting your bodyweight up as much as possible before setting yourself all the way down into the pose.

7. Start walking your chest up the fabric into an arched back.
8. Push the tails away from your body and split.

(REMINDER:)

TO EXIT: Hold high onto your free pole, lean back and release the top leg. Simultaneously grab the working pole. From there you can hold both poles and let the tails unravel below you.

pg 67

47. CANDY CANE CROSSBACK
FROM AN INVERTED CRUCIFIX WRAP

REMINDER:
A similar look to the traditional Crossback Straddle but a different entry which allows for greater split mobility. During the entry there is potential to fall out so please be mindful of the steps.

1. Split the poles with your body in the center, pull up and straddle invert.
2. Crochete each leg, from the outside in around each pole.
3. Legs should straighten up the fabric and toes should be turned inward over the fabric to create grip.

Do not FULLY let go of the fabric with your hands at any point until both fabrics are fully crossed behind you and brought back to the front.

STRADDLE INVERT - LEGS TO THE OUTSIDE
BODY IN BETWEEN POLES BEFORE INVERTING
CROCHETE LEG AND ANKLE AROUND EACH POLE
TURN TOES INWARD TO GRIP THE FABRIC
BRING POLES DOWN BEHIND YOUR BACK
CROSS THE POLES BEHIND YOUR BACK
BRING THE POLES BACK TO THE FRONT

4. Place each pole behind your lower back and cross them. Meaning switch each pole into the opposite hand. This creates an 'X' with the fabric at your back.
5. Once the poles are crossed bring them back to the front of your body.

tip: Sliding down is common for beginners when trying to cross the fabrics. Keep as much tension on the poles as possible and grip your feet as tight as you can.

pg 68

6. Bring your right leg out of the fabric by bending it down as if you were going to touch your nose to your knee.
7. Place the right fabric tail against your INNER THIGH and then over your leg completely.
8. Crochete your leg back in and pull your fabric taut.

> tip: Keep the fabric taut through the whole process.

BRING RIGHT LEG OUT BY BENDING KNEE TO NOSE

FABRIC GOES TO INNER THIGH AND THEN OVER ENTIRE LEG

CROCHETE LEG BACK IN AND PULL FABRIC TAUT

REPEAT ON OTHER SIDE BUT CONTINUE THE WRAP ALL THE WAY DOWN TO THE ANKLE

WRAP ALL THE WAY DOWN TO THE ANKLE

9. Pull the left leg out and repeat the process BUT continue wrapping the tail all the way down to the ankle.
10. Once the wraps are done on the left, keep that leg out. Pull the right leg back out and wrap the tails all the way down to the ankle on the right side.
11. With both wraps complete you can now let go and hang in your crossback.

PULL OUT RIGHT LEG AND WRAP ALL THE WAY DOWN TO THE ANKLE

FULLY EXTEND INTO A STRADDLE

REMINDER:

TO EXIT: Simply reach up, grab the top poles and sit up. Point your toes to the floor and the fabric will begin to unravel.

48. CANDY CANE TILT

FROM A CANDY CANE X BACK

REMINDER:

TO EXIT: Lower back into a crossback hang and exit as you would from a Candy Cane X Back.

REACH UP FOR YOUR LEFT LEG

GRAB LEFT ANKLE WITH RIGHT HAND

FEED LEFT HAND THROUGH AND BRACE AGAINST FABRIC

1. Start in a Candy Cane Crossback (pg 68)
2. Reach over towards your left leg, hold onto your left ankle with your right hand.
3. Reach through with your left hand towards the poles and grab the poles.
4. Drop your other leg down to the ground and allow your body to tilt down to the ground.

tip

It can be difficult to control your tilt from going too far, be sure to brace yourself against the pole of the fabric with your free arm!

49. SLING SPLIT - MIDDLE
FROM A LOOPED TAIL HOLD

tip: Staying put while re-gripping the fabric can be a big challenge in this pose. Be sure to keep one grip super secure while releasing the hand to regrip the other tail.

REMINDER: TO EXIT: Bend your knees and sink back down to the starting position. One by one release the tail and regrip just the pole.

INVERT BETWEEN POLES THEN SPLIT LEGS TO FRONT OF POLES

HOOK KNEES OVER POLES

BRING THE BASE TAIL UP TOGETHER IN A TIGHT GRIP WITH THE TOP POLE

LIFT UP CHEST AND PUSH OUT INTO A MIDDLE SPLIT

1. Invert between the poles. Keep your legs between the poles when you invert.
2. Hook your knees over the front of the poles.

tip: Make sure to get the pole set deeply into the knee pit and squeeze tightly.

3. Take the tail under your right knee pit and bring it up to meet the top right pole.
4. Grip both the tail and the top pole together. Best to use a thumb facing up grip.
5. Do this with both sides.
6. Pull your chest up and straddle into a middle split. Sometimes hand placement can make a difference in how easy or hard it is to lift up.

tip: The closer your hands to your knees the harder it will be to balance.

pg 71

50. SLING SPLIT - FRONT
FROM A LOOPED TAIL HOLD

tip: I recommend pushing your loops down past the knees for a front split. Also holding your grip higher up the fabric will help create a better balance here.

HIGH HAND GRIP ON POLES

ROTATE BACK KNEE DOWN AND TWIST HIPS

1. From a Sling Middle Split (pg 70) push the loops out past the knees so they are sitting either below or slightly above the calf muscle.

tip: This is best done by leaning back to bring the legs together in front of you and then using your feet to push each loop down each leg. Keep your hand grip high to help with this.

2. Decide which leg will be your back leg and rotate it down towards the ground.
3. Keep your chest up and hold a split position.

REMINDER:

TO EXIT: It will be best to slide the loops back to your knees first and then sink back into an inverted knee hook. Like how you began.

51. SHOULDER SLING SPLIT

FROM A LOOPED TAIL HOLD

tip: Controlling the tension and getting the fabric down to the ankles without losing it will be your challenge for this pose! Try to keep the fabric taut and squeeze the poles tightly with the shoulders while entering into the pose.

INVERT BETWEEN POLES THEN SPLIT LEGS IN FRONT OF POLES

HOOK KNEES OVER POLES

PICK UP TAIL AND LAY OVER SHOULDER

SQUEEZE TAIL WITH SHOULDERS AND SPLIT LEGS

SHIMMY FABRIC DOWN TO ANKLES

SPLIT OUT

1. Invert between the poles. Keep your legs between the poles when you invert.
2. Hook your knees over the front of the poles.

tip: Make sure to get the pole set deeply into the knee pit and squeeze tightly.

3. Take the tail under your right knee pit and bring it up over your right shoulder. Be sure it lays from the front of your chest over to your back.
4. Do this with both sides.
5. Pull your chest up and straddle, from here use your opposite foot to help push the fabric down to the ankle or calf muscle.

tip: The closer your hands to your knees the harder it will be to balance.

pg 73

52. THIGH HITCH LAYBACK SPLIT

FROM A THIGH HITCH WRAP

REMINDER:

This pose has alot of wraps, it would be very easy to lose sense of direction and get tangled up. I recommend only doing this when you have an instructor present to walk you through the EXIT. You have to reverse all the steps which can get confusing.

1. Invert with the fabric running along your right side and crochete your right leg.
2. Bend your right knee over the fabric while simultaneously reaching up with your left hand.

tip The model shows a right crochete wrap with her left hand high. However I have found having the right hand high with a right leg crochete can be a little more fluid as you release to regrip above your knee.

RIGHT SIDE INVERT

RIGHT SIDE CROCHETE

BEND RIGHT KNEE AND REACH UP

PULL BODY UP AND KEEP THIGH CLOSE TOGETHER

3. Grip the fabric above your knee with both hands and begin to pull your body up.

tip Touch your inner thighs together as you do this to prevent sliding down the fabric.

pg 74

PULL UP AND STRAIGHTEN LEGS

KEY OVER

GRAB LEFT POLE WITH LEFT HAND

SLIDE RIGHT ARM AND BODY BETWEEN POLES

4. Pull your body upright, straighten your legs and key over the fabric.
5. Split the poles with your left hand and slide your right hand through.

(tip) It does matter which pole you grab, if you make an unneccessary/extra twist in the poles or it will make everything tighter. Rule of thumb grab the natural left side pole with your left hand.

FOLD SLIGHTLY AND CONTINUE SLIDING BODY THROUGH

LEFT HIP ROTATES UP AND OVER TO A SEATED POSITION

6. Continue to slide your body through and then rotate your hips over into a seated position.

(tip) Keep your shoulders low and drive your legs high in order to have a smooth rotation.

BRING FREE LEG OUT

7. Grip both hands onto the left pole.
8. Scoot your bottom back so the fabric slides down to the knee and remove your free leg.

(tip) You must grab the left pole. That is the pole to the left side of you when you are seated.

PASS FREE LEG UNDER YOUR POLE

CONTINUE ALL THE WAY THROUGH

PLACE LEFT ELBOW OVER POLE

TURN YOUR BACK INTO THE FABRIC

9. Pass your free leg completely under the pole you are holding onto.
10. Simultaneously place your left elbow over the pole you are holding and turn your back into and against the same pole.

tip This motion directly mimicks the roll up used in Mermaid Split (pg 31)

11. Pull your left knee up to your chest and grab your ankle.
12. Lean back and straighten out your left leg into a full split.

tip Be sure your left leg stay on the outside of your pole or you won't be able to do the pose.

53. THIGH HITCH KNEE HANG SPLIT

FROM A THIGH HITCH WRAP

REMINDER:
This wrap applies alot of pressure to the knee so please be cautious.
TO EXIT: Reach back up for the fabric and sit up, DO NOT let go of your tail until you have sat back up. Unravel the tail and complete the typical exit you would for a thigh hitch.

RIGHT SIDE INVERT

RIGHT SIDE CROCHETE

BEND RIGHT KNEE AND REACH UP

PULL BODY UP AND KEEP THIGH CLOSE TOGETHER

1. Invert with the fabric running along your right side and crochete your right leg.
2. Bend your right knee over the fabric while simultaneously reaching up with your left hand.

> **tip** The model shows a right crochete wrap with her left hand high. However I have found having the right hand high with a right leg crochete can be a little more fluid as you release to regrip above your knee.

3. Grip the fabric above your knee with both hands and begin to pull your body up.

> **tip** Touch your inner thighs together as you do this to prevent sliding down the fabric.

pg 77

PULL UP STRAIGHTEN UP AND KEY OVER

FABRIC GETS WRAPPED FROM THE OUTSIDE IN

REPEAT 2-3 TIMES

4. Once your body is up high straighten your left leg and key over to your right.
5. Grab the tail and begin to wrap it down the leg. The wrap goes under and around the back of your thigh before coming up and between the thighs.
6. Wrap the tail 2-3 times.

{tip} The direction of your wrap is important. Start by taking the tail to the outside of the thigh, around the back of the thigh and then into the middle towards your body.

UNFOLD SO YOUR BODY DROPS DOWN

HANG FROM THE KNEE

ROTATE HIPS AND KNEE OUT AWAY FROM YOU

PULL ON FABRIC, ARCH UP AND SPLIT

7. Bend the right knee and allow your body to unkey and drop down towards the floor. The wraps will cinch up towards the knee pit as you drop down.
8. Keep your knee bent, take the tail and twist your body so that you are in a backbend holding the tail above your head.
9. Once there simply pull on the tail to arch as much as possible and straighten both legs out into a full split.

{tip} The twisting motion may feel akward in the beginning. In order to complete this your hips must rotate to face the floor and your free leg's knee must also rotate to face the floor.

54. ALLEGRA
FROM A SCORPION WRAP

There is a point in this entry in which you can fall out easily. Please see the fall warning on the next page!

FABRIC ON THE RIGHT SIDE OF BODY

CROCHETE RIGHT LEG

REACH LEFT HAND DOWN FOR FABRIC

WRAP TAIL TO THE INSIDE OF THIGH AND OVER

CONTINUE WRAP ALL THE WAY DOWN TO ANKLE

1. Invert with the fabric running along the right side of your body.

tip Keep the same side arm highest on your grip. So right hand higher than left hand on the pole.

2. Crochete your right leg around the top pole.
3. Release your left hand and reach down for the tail running behind your back.
4. Grab the tail, lift it up over the inner thigh and around the leg.
5. Repeat the wrap all the way down to your ankle. Typically 3-4 wraps.

pg 79

MOVE WRAPPED LEG TO A BENT POSITION BEHIND YOUR BACK

GRAB AND STRAIGHTEN TOP LEG WITH SAME SIDE ARM

RELEASE TENSION ON BACK LEG

6. Move your wrapped leg so that it is now bent behind you in a backbend.
7. Then bend the top knee so that it is hooked over the pole of the fabric.
9. Hold onto the tail loosely and allow your back leg to
move freely as needed in order to complete the next step.
10. Grab onto the outside of your calf muscle and straighten your leg out. Proceed to move your hand to the ankle as your leg straightens.
12. From there extend fully into the pose.

You can release your TAIL briefly to use both hands to get your grip high on the fabric.

You must understand that your top leg's thigh is a brace against the fabric. This stops you from falling out of the pose. If your top leg were to fall away from you to the back side of the pole you could fall out. Please make sure you understand this concept thoroughly before doing this pose high.

55. ALLEGRA UNBOUND

FROM A SCORPION WRAP

The same pose as Allegra (pg 78) however your release your back leg to achieve a full split

You must understand that your top leg's thigh is a brace against the fabric. This stops you from falling out of the pose. If your top leg were to fall away from you to the back side of the pole you could fall out. Please make sure you understand this concept thoroughly before doing this pose high.

MOVE WRAPPED LEG TO A BENT POSITION BEHIND YOUR BACK

BRACE AGAINST THE POLE AND PULL OUT TOP LEG INTO A SPLIT

RELEASE TAIL AND STRAIGHTEN BOTTOM LEG

FULLY EXTEND

1. Follow the steps for Allegra (pg 78)
2. Move your wrapped leg so that it is now bent behind you in a backbend.
3. Then bend the top knee so that it is hooked over the pole of the fabric.
4. Release the tail but keep the leg bent behind you.
5. Grab onto the outside of your calf muscle and straighten your leg out. You can brace your other hand against the pole if this helps.
6. From there extend fully into the pose. Release back tail and straighten both legs.

56. JADE SPLIT ⚠️
INVERTED SINGLE LEG CROCHETE

REMINDER:

Jade split is hard on the hamstrings and is also a big balance move. Enter into it slowly to avoid pulling a muscle or dropping into it too quickly and falling forward.

1. Start with the fabric on your right side.
2. Straddle invert and crochete your left leg around the fabric. Hook your toes so you have a good grip against the pole of the fabric.

FABRIC ON THE RIGHT SIDE

CROCHETE LEFT LEG AROUND FABRIC

GRIP THE FABRIC WITH YOUR TOES

3. Continue holding on with your right hand. Release your left hand and reach down below your head for the fabric.

tip: Naturally you want to put your hand behind your back for the fabric, however, it will be faster if you simply point your arm down to the ground by your head. Your tail naturally falls straight down so if you mimick that with your arm you will be able to find the tail quite quickly.

HOLD ON WITH YOUR RIGHT ARM

LEFT HAND GRABS TAIL

PULL FABRIC BEHIND YOUR BACK AND TO THE LEFT SIDE

4. Pull the fabric behind your back and to the other side.

tip: At this point you can release your right hand but you must keep holding on with your left.

5. Keep the fabric wrapping around your back and bring it to your front.
6. Bring your free leg (right leg) in and bend your knee.
7. Place your right foot into the tail of the fabric and then switch hands so you are holding the tail with your right hand.
8. Slowly relase your top leg and extend it down into a split. Watch your balance so you don't tip too far.

⚠️

Do not let go of the fabric with your right hand or let your right foot slip out of the tail. ALSO be aware that you using the correct sides for everything. Starting with the fabric on wrong side or hooking the wrong foot will cause you to fall. TO EXIT: Grab the tail by your hip with the same side hand and regrip the top pole with the other hand. The tail will fall off your foot during this process, make sure your grip is secure. You can either re-hook your top leg or allow your body to rotate upright, hold on tight.

57. JADED DANCERS ⚠️
FROM JADE SPLIT

⚠️

The same warnings/reminders for the above Jade Split apply to these poses aswell.

1. From a regular Jade Split (pg 82) reach your same side arm behind you. If your left leg is behind you then your left arm will reach back.
2. Bend your knee and grab your ankle or the top of your foot and extend out.
3. Your front foot will tip upward, just do the motion slow and controlled so as not tip too far forward.

58. CAN OPENER
FROM A JADE SPLIT

REMINDER:

This pose requires alot of fabric awareness and manipulation. It is hard to keep the pole hooked correctly around your back leg split. THE EXIT for this is also precarious and should be addressed by your coach. You will need to make sure you have a good grip on your live end before unravelling the tail. You are basically exiting as you would a Jade Split. You just have more fabric to deal with.

tip

I have found some people even like to put the fabric between their toes to help keep it in place during the end stages.

The same warnings/reminders for Jade Split on the previous page apply to these poses aswell.

START POSITION FROM JADE SPLIT

TAKE TAIL AROUND THE BACK AND TO THE FRONT OF THE BODY

FABRIC GOES FROM THE INSIDE OVER THE SOLE OF THE FOOT

1. Start in a Jade Split entry (pg 82) pause once the tail is hooked around your foot.
2. Instead of releasing your top leg like a Jade Split keep your top leg wrapped.
3. Take the tail of the fabric and wrap it behind your back and to the front of your body.
4. One the tail has been completely wrapped around the body bring your top leg down by bending the knee in towards your chest deeply.
5. Place the tail against your INNER calf/foot then wrap it over the sole of your foot.

pg 84

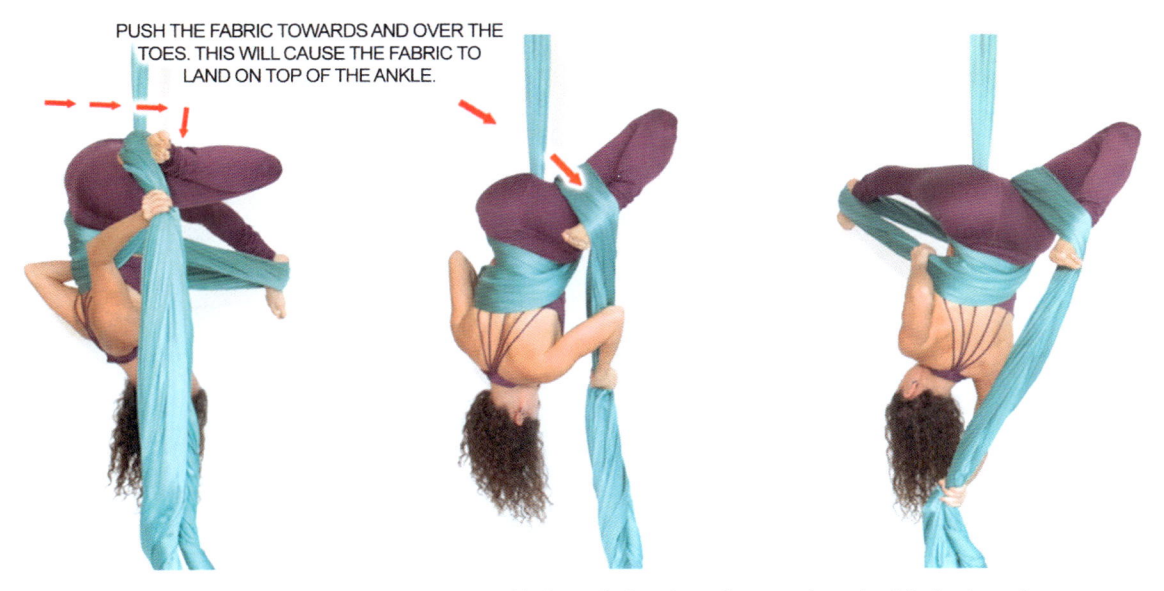

PUSH THE FABRIC TOWARDS AND OVER THE TOES. THIS WILL CAUSE THE FABRIC TO LAND ON TOP OF THE ANKLE.

6. Now here's where it gets a little tricky, begin to slowly kick that leg behind you but STOP about halfway.
7. From here you are going to SWITCH the fabric with your hands so it just lays flat over the top of your foot.

!tip You do not have to do this but I feel it makes the wrap prettier.

STRAIGHTEN AND GENTLY GUIDE FABRIC OFF OF YOUR KNEE

8. Once you have adjusted the fabric at your ankle you can begin to slowly push out into a full split.
9. As you push out into your split your fabric may get caught over your knee. You'll want to SLOWLY straighten your leg to kick the fabric off the knee.

!tip If you pull too tight on your fabric during this motion it will ride up back leg and not cascade down straight.

59. WINE GLASS
FROM A JADE SPLIT

> **REMINDER:**
> Exiting requires a thorough awareness of wrap theory/jade split theory. You need to be holding your main tails to keep you locked in while unravelling the back leg. This is best shown in person by an instructor, please see your coach for proper exit etiquette.

1. Review Can Opener entry (pg 84) and stop once your tail has been wrapped around your lower back and pulled to the front. Like the first position shown here.

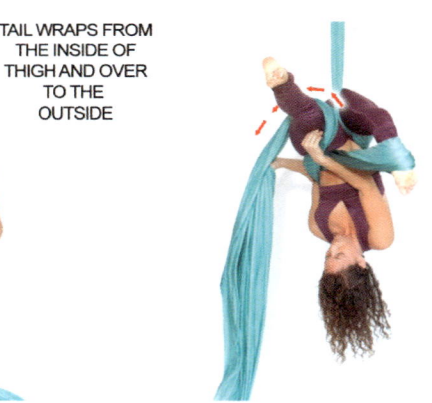

2. Bend your free leg into your chest and begin to wrap the fabric over your leg all the way down your thigh to your ankle. Note the direction of the wrap goes from the inside to outside

TAIL WRAPS FROM THE INSIDE OF THIGH AND OVER TO THE OUTSIDE

CONTINUE THE WRAP ALL THE WAY DOWN TO YOUR ANKLE

pg 86

3. Once your leg is fully wrapped, hold onto your tail and begin to open up into a full split.

> tip Try to achieve a fairly full balanced Jade Split first before moving onto the next step.

4. Allow your front leg to tilt up and rest against the pole of the fabric.

5. Do this SLOWLY and keep your top foot slightly pointed so that the fabric does not slip off of your toes as you rest it against the pole of the fabric.

The one thing you really want to be mindful of is keeping the fabric firmly pressed against the sole of the top foot! You don't want it to slip off the toes!

pg 87

60. OPEN POLE JADE SPLIT

FROM A JADE SPLIT SET UP

REMINDER:

This is a very precarious pose. Not keeping track of which tail is your weight bearing tail can cause you to fall. You really need to have a thorough understanding of Jade Wrap Theory! Please have your coach review or be there to guide you through this pose.

1. Review Jade Split entry (pg 82) and stop once your tail has been set around the sole of your foot. Like the first position shown below.
2. Release your top leg, bend the knee and rest it down close to your chest.
3. Currently both tails are set against the sole of your front foot, CAREFULLY take ONE of those tails off and place it against the sole of the other foot.
4. Now you have one tail on each foot.

⚠️ Do not AT ANY POINT in this whole pose, lose the tail, tension and hold on the front foot of your Jade Split.

INITIAL JADE SPLIT STARTING POSITION

BEND TOP LEG DOWN

SPLIT POLES SO ONE TAIL IS AGAINST EACH FOOT

MAIN FOOT

(tip) The FRONT foot tail (not the bent leg) is your MAIN tail and what you should be focused on holding. If you lose your front tail then you will fall out. However your back tail is perfectly okay to let go of.

HOLD ONTO BOTH TAILS AND PUSH BACK LEG INTO A SPLIT

5. Hold onto both tails and begin to push your back foot out into a split.

> **tip** You must still maintain BALANCE in this pose. Your weight and how well you hold the pose is still centered around your front foot tail. The back tail is simply aesthetics.

WALK YOUR ARMS AND CHEST DOWN THE FABRIC

THE FURTHUR YOU CAN WALK YOUR HANDS INTO THE BACK LEG POLE THE BETTER YOUR TRIANGLE WILL LOOK

6. Your front foot will rise up slightly which is okay as long as you don't go too far.
7. Look down to the ground and begin to adjust your tails so they make a triangle shape.
8. Holding the poles and your hands further away from your head towards the ground will also create a better triangle than shown here.

> **tip**

It takes practice to perfect the shape, have your coach help guide you into the best shape.

61. S-WRAP DANCER SPLIT
FROM A JADE SPLIT SET UP

tip

This pose is performed while in an S-Wrap, and can be a great pose before continuing into other S-Wrap actions like drops etc.. However I actually show the entry to this pose from a Jade Split because it's better described with images!

REMINDER:

TO EXIT you can continue into any S-wrap based pose or back into a Jade Split and exit from there.

FRONT LEG PASSES FORWARD BEYOND THE POLE

GRAB BASE LEG AND EXTEND

1. Review Jade Split entry (pg 82) and stop once your tail has been set around the sole of your foot. Like the first position shown above.
2. Do not let go of your tail, allow your top leg to pass forward past the pole of the fabric.

tip If right leg was the front splitting leg then fabric passes to the right side of the pole.

3. Try to keep your foot high up towards the ceiling. Otherwise it's easy for your foot to twist off to the side.
4. Grab your back leg and extend into a split/dancer pose.

pg 90

62. SINGLE HIP HANG SPLIT

FROM AN OUTSIDE LEG CROCHETE

REMINDER:
You could injur your elbow here so do not lock out your elbow. This is also an extreme strain on the front leg hamstring, practice low and stretch first. TO EXIT hook your front leg back over the pole (crochete if posible) and then grip the pole with both hands and straddle out to lower.

tip
You must keep your right arm strong and engaged after regripping. Do not let your elbow hyper extend. The weight of your body rests in the sling created by your hip crease fabric and right hand hold.

LEFT LEG WILL CROCHETE
TAIL RUNS ALONG RIGHT SIDE
KNEE COMES FORWARD
SWITCH GRIP SO THUMB POINTS UP
EXTEND RIGHT LEG FORWARD AND GRAB WITH LEFT HAND

1. Keep the fabric on your right side, invert and crochete your left leg over the pole.
2. Make sure your toe grip is tight, and pull your right knee forward.
3. Release with your right hand only, grab the tail of the fabric with thumbs facing up.
4. Wedge the fabric into your hip crease, and then begin to release the left hand so that your body sets down into the fabric on the hip crease.

RELEASE YOUR TOP LEG
VIEW FLIP
LOWER INTO SPLIT

5. Take the left hand and grip your right foot thats extended out in front of you.
6. Release the top left leg and slowly extend it out into a split.

Extend into a split very slowly, if you go to fast you could throw yourself off balance. This pose requires an extreme amount of grip strength. Lack of grip training and strength could cause you to fall easily.

pg 91

63. CLOSED FLOATING SPLIT

FROM AN OUTSIDE LEG CROCHETE

REMINDER:

This pose is all about grip strength. Please train your grip and practice safely. TO EXIT: Bend your top leg, crunch into a ball so that your booty sinks back down to the floor. Regrip so that you can straddle invert to exit OR if your grip is strong enough you release your bottom hand while in the pose. Everything will unravel and you will be holding on with only the top hand.

1. Straddle invert with the fabric on the right side of your body, hook your left knee over the pole of the fabric.   *tip* Start with the left hand above the right in your initial invert.

2. Re-grip high up on the pole with your left hand.

⚠ Do not let go with your right base hand at any point during this pose. Everything will unravel and your only point of contact will be your top hand.

3. Lift your body up high and begin to turn your hips into the fabric so that your left leg slides all the way over the pole.
4. Belly should be facing out and down to the floor, back leg is up in an arabesque position.
5. Arch your back as much as possible and extend your front leg as far forward as possible.

64. OPEN FLOATING SPLIT

FROM AN INSIDE LEG CROCHETE

REMINDER:

This is another pose that requires great strength and fabric awareness. This is not a secure or locked hold. Be mindful of your foot transitions. TO EXIT: Release your right foot and instantly knee hook over the pole. Keep in mind If you miss you will fall.

1. Straddle invert with fabric on the right.
2. Hook your right knee.
3. Reach down with your left hand for the fabric tails.
4. Hold tails together tightly at your hip bone.

tip Make sure there is no slack behind your back once you have gripped the tails at your hip bone.

5. Bring your left foot up to the top pole and press it against the pole.

tip Use this as leverage to press into the pole and release your right leg.

6. Bring your right leg forward into your right hand grip.
7. Release your left leg back down into a split.

The transitions with your feet can be tricky and are not secure holds. Be mindful not to let your top foot slip off before you are ready. Your hand grip is also extremely vital! Practice safely!

65. HAND BALANCE SPLIT ⚠️

FROM AN INSIDE LEG CROCHETE

REMINDER:

There are alot of factors at play here to keep your balance. Having a good split will make a huge difference in this pose. TO EXIT: Release your top leg and hook the knee back over the poles. Regrip the fabric with your right hand and exit out the way you came.

FABRIC ON RIGHT | **RIGHT KNEE HOOK** | **LEFT HAND DOWN TO TAILS** | **TAIL GOES BEHIND SHOULDER THEN OVER ARMPIT** | **WRAP TAIL 2-3 TIMES** | **THUMBS DOWN GRIP**

1. **Straddle invert with fabric on your right, hook your right knee over the poles.**

   💡 *tip* Start with the left hand above the right in your initial invert.

2. **Reach your left hand down for the tails, pass the tail behind your shoulder then up over the armpit.**

   ⚠️ The direction in which the tails wraps is very important. If wrapped in the other direction you will fall out. The initial wrap should run behind the shoulder and then under the armpit first.

3. **Wrap the tails down the arm 2-3 times.**

   💡 *tip* Hand grip on the tails should be thumbs facing down.

pg 94

LEGS PULL FORWARD STRADDLING POLES

RIGHT HAND GRIPS RIGHT FOOT

SLOWLY LOWER BACK LEG INTO SPLIT

4. Shift your weight by bringing both legs forward. As if you were going to touch both knees to your nose.

⚠️ The fabric pole must be in between your legs. Do not whatsoever let your whole right leg fall away from the poles or you will fall. Both legs are essentially straddling the pole of the fabric.

5. Grip your right foot with your right hand.

💬(tip) Keep tension on your right foot. You must stay actively engaged and keep your hand grip and front foot pulled low.

6. Very slowly extend your left leg back into a split. Watch your balance. You must stay actively engaged.

66. HANDSTAND MIDDLE SPLIT
FROM AN INSIDE LEG CROCHETE

REMINDER:

This pose requires alot of balance and body awareness to complete. Practice low until you have mastered this skill. TO EXIT: Crochete each leg seperately around its correlating pole. Keep your toe grip tight and unravel the arms to regrip.

FABRIC ON RIGHT

RIGHT CROCHETE

LEFT LEG CROSSES OVER FOR EXTRA GRIP

SPLIT TAILS

HEAD IN BETWEEN TAILS

TAILS TO THE FRONT

1. Straddle invert with fabric on your right, crochete your right leg up around the top pole.

tip Place and squeeze your left leg over the top crochete aswell. Squeeze tightly. This will help you from sliding as you work with your tails.

2. Spread the tails so that you have one tail on each side of your body.
3. Each tail needs to run behind its correlating shoulder blade and then brought together in front of you.

Keep as much tension on your foot crochete as possible. Beause you are adjusting your tails alot in this pose it can be easy to lose grip and fall or slide.

NOTE THE TAIL RUNNING BEHIND THE SHOULDER

4. Hold onto both tails with one hand, proceed to wrap the other arm around the tail two times and then grip with a thumbs facing down grip.

tip Get the first wraps as high up on your arms as possible. Make sure the wraps are fairly even.

5. Repeat with the other arm.

There is fall potential here. The direction the tails wrap must be correct. The tails must run along the back side of your shoulder, to the inside of your neck then up and over your armpit.

ADJUST ARMS INTO HANDSTAND POSITION

BEND YOUR KNEES OFF AND AWAY FROM THE FABRIC

SLOWLY STRADDLE OUT INTO A MIDDLE SPLIT

6. Once wrapped, bring your arms into a handstand position. Actively engage your arms and stay strong.
7. Slowly bend your knees down and away from the fabric.

tip Use this moment to find your balance point. The best balance comes when your feet stay slightly forward of your body. Much like a piked straddle.

8. Continue to straddle your legs out into a middle split.

This is quite a serious balance. Sudden motions will throw you off and out of the pose. The tension of the tails at the hips feels as if you are being pushed off the fabric. Counter this by bringing your toes/legs slightly more forward.

67. HANDSTAND SPLIT THROUGH
FROM AN INSIDE LEG CROCHETE

REMINDER:

This pose requires all the same strength a handstand on the floor would require plus aerial awareness strength. You must be comfortable in handstands on the floor. TO EXIT: Put your head down, push into your arms and drive your legs back up to the top poles. Crochete your legs for grip then unravel your arms. To regrip and exit.

BRACE RIGHT FOOT

KEEP YOUR TOE GRIP BUT LET HIP SLIDE THROUGH

REPEAT

HIPS SLIE THROUGH

RELEASE LEFT LEG

HEAD UP AND ARCH

ENGAGE AND PUSH ARMS DOWN

1. From a Handstand Middle Split (pg 96) bend your right knee and hook your right toes around the right fabric pole.

tip The right leg hook is meant to brace yourself in a semi-sturdy position as you adjust your left leg into its proper place.

2. Move your left leg up to the left pole. Let your whole left leg and hip slide gently through the poles. Keep your left toes flexed so they DO NOT pass to the other side. Instead they should brace you against the pole.
3. Unhook your right foot and repeat.
4. Hips should be in the center of pole and the toe grip is the only thing keeping you balanced.

⚠ Positioning yourself between the fabric with only your toes holding you up is difficult and it is very easy to slip and fall. Move cautiously.

5. From there release, ONLY your left leg and point it down to the floor in a split position.

tip To achieve the best shape drive your arms down to the floor while arching your back and lifting your head up.

68. STRAIGHTJACKET SPLIT
FROM A DOUBLE LEG CROCHETE

REMINDER: This pose is extremely strenuous on your shoulders! Tight shoulders will be your enemy here. Practice low!

1. Start out in a traditional double leg crochete.
2. From there, bring the fabric close together behind you.
3. Switch your grip so that your right hand is holding the left tail and your left hand is holding the right tail.

STRADDLE INVERT

DOUBLE LEG CROCHETE

tip DO NOT cross your fabric tails. Only your arms.

CROSS HAND GRIP BUT DO NOT CROSS TAILS

SLOWLY RELEASE LEGS AND SPLIT OUT

4. Thumbs should be in an upward facing grip.
5. Slowly release and straddle your legs.

tip To achieve the flat plank position like the very top right image, allow your booty to sink over your arms and arch your back. This does require alot of core strength.

This pose requires alot of grip strength. Poor grip training could cause you fall and injur yourself.

pg 99

69. MISSION IMPOSSIBLE ⚠️
FROM A DOUBLE CROCHETE

REMINDER:

This pose takes an extreme amount of strength in the outer thighs. As well in the arms/hamstrings once in position. Doing abductor exercises will help prepare you for this pose. TO EXIT: Simply lean back upside down and straddle out.

⚠️

If you fall forward, hold on tightly with your hands You will do a flip but as long as you hold on with your hands you will not fall to the floor.

DOUBLE CROCHETE SLIDE FEET DOWN

PULL CHEST UPWARDS

DRIVE CHEST FORARD

DRIVE LIMBS OUTWARDS

1. Start in a double leg crochete, then bend your knees and slide your toes down the fabric.
2. Pull your chest up and crunch into a ball.

> (tip) This whole process is best done in one full and fluid motion.

3. Throw your chest forward while driving your arms and legs out to the side.

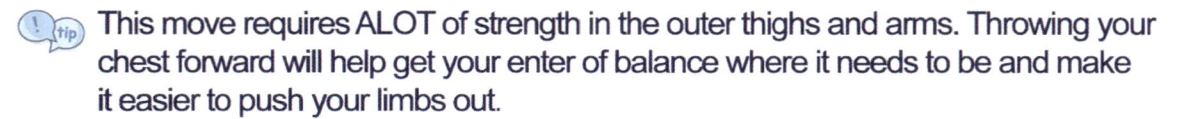

> (tip) This move requires ALOT of strength in the outer thighs and arms. Throwing your chest forward will help get your enter of balance where it needs to be and make it easier to push your limbs out.

4. Press into your arms and legs to sit up striaight in your middle split.

> (tip) Some people prefer to start this whole process with an extra wrist wrap like model shows. However the wrist wrap can make your exit more difficult.

CHAPTER FIVE
POSES FROM A BELAY LOOP

Welcome to Chapter Five, here you will find poses that stem from a Belay Loop. A thorough understanding of Belay Loops is required. This is something you must truly understand before doing these poses. You must be able to recognize your live end and understand how it works within your Belay Loop. Not understanding your live end and your belay entries/exits could cost you serious injury.

pg 102

pg 103

pg 104

pg 105

pg 106

pg 107

pg 108

pg 109

pg 110

pg 111

pg 112

pg 113

pg 114

pg 116

pg 101

70. DANCER IN BELAY
FROM A BELAY WRAP & SINGLE FOOTLOCK

REMINDER:
Keep weight in the loop as you do this. If you stand upright too much the pressure from the live end will suck the loop in and shrink it.

SINGLE LEG FOOTLOCK WITH TAILS TOGETHER

SAME SIDE ARM, GRAB ANKLE AND EXTEND

1. From Belay do a Single Footlock on your tails.
   tip Keep both tails together as one whole piece.

2. Position the Belay Loop just under your shoulder blades.

3. Grab your free ankle with the same side hand and extend out into a Dancer Split.

71. SPLIT LAYBACK
FROM A BELAY WRAP & SINGLE FOOTLOCK

Be careful not to tilt too far or your footlock tail will begin to slide into the belay knot and disappear! If you are not aware of this and it happens it could cause you to fall out of the loop.

NOTE POTENTIAL FOR TAIL GAP TO SINK IN IF YOU INVERT FURTHUR

FABRIC ON LOWER BACK - BACK IS JUST SLIGHTLY BELOW LEVEL WITH BELAY LOOP

1. From Belay, do a single footlock around both tails together.
2. Lower the Belay loop to your lower back.
3. Lift your free leg up and grab your ankle with your same side arm.
4. Lay back and split into position one, where the legs are in a full split and your back is just slightly below your Belay Loop.
5. You can choose to go furthur but be cautious and heed the fall warning.

72. ARMPIT HANG FRONT SPLIT
FROM A BELAY WITH DOUBLE FOOTLOCKS

REMINDER:

Positioning your body well below your knot BEFORE you start your double footlocks will help to keep your footlocks even.

tip

Before getting into this one make sure to lengthen your Belay Loop so that your head sits lower than the Belay Knot. This will help your pose look much better and stop your from getting crunched by your Belay Loop. The further under the better.

HEAD SHOULD BE EVEN FURTHER BELOW KNOT

DOUBLE WRAP

1. Once in Belay, release your legs, split your tails and do a Double Footlock.

2. Make sure your Belay Loop is adjusted so your head sits UNDER your Belay Knot and then open up into a Left or Right Front Split.

COMPLETE DOUBLE FOOTLOCKS

ONCE COMPLETE, OPEN INTO A SPLIT

pg 104

73. SHOULDER HANG MIDDLE SPLIT
FROM A BELAY WITH DOUBLE FOOTLOCKS

REMINDER:

Positioning your body well below your knot BEFORE you start your double footlocks will help to keep your footlocks even.

tip

Before getting into this one make sure to lengthen your Belay Loop so that your head sits lower than the Belay Knot This will help your pose look much better and stop you from getting crunched by your Belay Loop. The further under the better.

HEAD SHOULD BE EVEN FURTHER BELOW KNOT

DOUBLE WRAP

1. Once in Belay, release your legs, split your tails and do a Double Footlock.
2. Make sure your Belay Loop is adjusted so your head sits UNDER the Knot and then open up into a Middle Split.

COMPLETE DOUBLE FOOTLOCKS

ONCE COMPLETE, OPEN INTO A SPLIT

74. CONTORTION PANCAKE
FROM A BELAY WRAP & DOUBLE FOOTLOCK

REMINDER:
Like many other Belay poses this one is all about getting the right ratio of Belay Loop size and even Footlocks. This may take a few tries to learn where the best position for your Loop and Locks are.

ACHIEVE A SMALL LOOP AND EVEN FOOTLOCKS IN A MIDDLE SPLIT

LOOP ON LOWER BACK AND BEGIN TO ARCH OVER

INNER THIGHS FACE UP AND LOOP STAYS ON LOWER BACK

1. Similar to a Shoulder Hang Middle Split (pg 105) cinch up your loop and adjust your locks so that you are fairly close to your Belay Knot.
2. Position Belay Loop so that it is on your lower back.
3. Arch over your loop and allow your legs to invert slightly.

tip: You should not invert all the way. Your inner thighs in your middle split should be facing straight up to the ceiling.

4. You want to accentuate your back arch, hence the contortion pose, by leaving the fabric above your tailbone on your lower back.

75. HAND HANG SPLIT
FROM A BELAY WRAP & SFL ON BOTH TAILS

REMINDER:

It's all in the grip for this pose! Make sure you place the back of your wrist in the Belay Loop and then close your hands over both sides of the loop together for a great grip.

1. From Belay, do a single footlock with BOTH tails together.

tip
The holding arm is the same side as footlock. So if you want to hold with your right arm then lock your right leg.

SLIDE THROUGH LOOP AND REGRIP WITH STRONG HAND

STRAIGHTEN OUT, GRIP THE FREE FOOT AND EXTEND INTO A SPLIT

2. Slide your body out of your Belay Loop, squat down to rest on your locked foot and wrap your holding hold into the Belay Loop.
3. Turn your body out to the side, begin to straighten you locked leg and grip your free foot with your free hand.
4. Extend out completely into a split.

The fall potential is in your grip strength, if you slip with your grip you will fall.

76. ELBOW HANG SPLIT
FROM A BELAY WRAP & SFL ON BOTH TAILS

REMINDER:

It's all in the grip for this pose! Make sure you place the elbow pit of your strong arm into the Belay Loop.

tip

Clenching your fist will help to tighten the forearm muscle allowing for extra grip in the pose.

⚠ The fall potential is from having a weak elbow grip, if you are not used to tolerating the pressure you could slip and fall.

1. From Belay, do a right single footlock with BOTH tails together.

tip

The holding arm is the same side as footlock. So if you want to hold with your right arm then lock your right leg.

SLIDE THROUGH LOOP AND REGRIP WITH ELBOW PIT

2. Slide your body out of your Belay Loop, squat down to rest on your locked foot.
3. Place your elbow pit into the Belay Loop.
4. Turn your body out to the side, straighten your locked leg and grip your free foot with your free hand.
5. Extend out completely into a split.

STRAIGHTEN OUT, GRIP THE FREE FOOT AND EXTEND INTO A SPLIT

pg 108

77. NECK HANG FRONT SPLIT
FROM A BELAY WRAP & DFL

DO NOT try this pose until you have spent time conditioning and preparing your neck for such an extreme pose. You should be cleared by your coach AND take into account any past injuries involving the neck and shoulders. THIS POSE CAN INJUR EASILY AND QUICKLY.

REMINDER:

Neck hangs of any kind are very dangerous! Please do not just try this pose on a whim or take it lightly. There are conditioning exercises and strength preps your instructor should be giving you to prepare as well as talking about and understanding alignment!

SLIDE THROUGH LOOP

GENTLY PLACE AT BASE OF SKULL

EXTEND INTO SPLIT

1. From Belay, enlarge your loop so that your whole body can easily slide through.
2. Once the loop is at a desired length, lock your feet into Double Footlocks.
3. Slide your body through and place the Belay Loop against the back of the neck just under the base of the skull.
3. IF you can release your hands here and feel comfortable then proceed to extending each leg into a split position.

THERE ARE ALIGNMENT do's and dont's. Have your coach clear you for such an intense and dangerous pose before trying.

77. NECK HANG MIDDLE SPLIT

FROM A BELAY WRAP & DFL

DO NOT try this pose until you have spent time conditioning and preparing your neck for such an extreme pose. You should be cleared by your coach AND take into account any past injuries involving the neck and shoulders. THIS POSE CAN INJUR EASILY AND QUICKLY.

REMINDER:

Neck hangs of any kind are very dangerous! Please do not just try this pose on a whim or take it lightly. There are conditioning exercises and strength preps your instructor should be giving you to prepare as well as talking about and understanding alignment!

SLIDE THROUGH LOOP

GENTLY PLACE AT BASE OF SKULL

EXTEND INTO SPLIT

1. From Belay, enlarge your loop so that your whole body can easily slide through.
2. Once the loop is at a desired length, lock your feet into Double Footlocks.
3. Slide your body through and place the Belay Loop against the back of the neck just under the base of the skull.
3. IF you can release your hands here and feel comfortable then proceed to extending each leg into a split position.

THERE ARE ALIGNMENT do's and dont's. Have your coach clear you for such an intense and dangerous pose before trying.

pg 110

79. HEXAGON
FROM A BELAY WRAP & INVERSION

REMINDER:

Keep an eye on your live end as this move tends to pull on it alot! It takes time and practice to perfect the shape of your hexagon. Practice with a mirror or have a spotter help you with learn the shape!

1. Rest your weight in your Belay Loop and split your tails.

   tip One tail on each side of your hip bones.

2. Invert and straddle all the way over until you can bring your legs close together the other side.

3. Seperate your tails and place each tail over the sole of each foot.

   tip Remember to keep lots of tension on your tails as your place your feet in so that they don't become uneven!

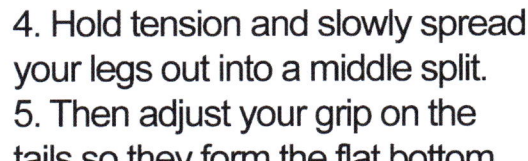

4. Hold tension and slowly spread your legs out into a middle split.
5. Then adjust your grip on the tails so they form the flat bottom of a hexagon.

80. KITE IN BELAY
FROM A BELAY WRAP & INVERSION

REMINDER:

This pose entry may feel similar to Hexagaon (pg 111) with one major difference. Your hips MUST be rotated to complete this pose. You want to think about having your back arched upon completion and your hips/belay loop almost turned sideways within the pose.

1. Hang with your back in Belay, your legs released and your tails split to each side of your hips.
2. Straddle Invert and bring your legs together around the other side of the poles.

ONE TAIL ON EACH SIDE OF HIPS

STRADDLE INVERT

BRING LEGS TO THE FRONT AND PLACE EACH TAIL OVER EACH SOLE OF FOOT

3. Split your tails and loop one tail against the sole of your front splitting foot.
4. Bend the free leg behind you and loop the other tail against the sole of the back splitting foot.

FABRIC AROUND SOLE OF BACK FOOT

FABRIC AROUND SOLE OF FRONT FOOT

EXTEND BOTH LEGS

5. Push through and extend both legs into a split.
6. Bring your tails together below you, arch your back and look towards your hands.

EXTEND ARMS AND BRING TAILS TOGETHER

ARCH YOUR BACK AND LOOK TO YOUR HANDS

81. DOUBLE LOOP SPLIT
FROM A BELAY WRAP & INVERSION

REMINDER:

When doing this pose be sure to lengthen your Belay Loop so that your head is sitting lower than your Belay Knot!

SPLIT TAILS OVER SOLE EACH FOOT

OPEN LEGS INTO A SPLIT AND REACH HANDS UP FOR POLES

JOIN TAILS WITH POLES

1. From a back hang in a Belay Loop, split your tails and loop each tail over the sole of each foot.

   tip Bending your knees first may help to get your feet in.

2. Holding onto your tails begin to split your legs and grab the two outer poles at the same time.

   tip You should have the tails and the poles in each grip.

pg 113

82. ANKLE HANG ARCHER

FROM AN ANKLE HANG IN BELAY

The biggest thing to be cautious with in this pose is your ankle hang. You should double wrap your ankle and you absolutely need to be mindful of the tension you are placing in the ankle. Too much pressure outwards or allowing the ankle to twist could cause it to come out! Practice with caution!!!!

STAND IN FOOTLOCK AND SLIDE OUT OF BELAY LOOP

KEEP TENSION ON LOOP

RAISE LEG

PLACE ANKLE IN LOOP AND DOUBLE WRAP LOOP AROUND ANKLE

1. Once in Belay, do a footlock around both pieces of fabric and slide your body out of the Belay Loop. Do not let go of the loop!
2. Lean back and place your ankle in the loop.

tip Keep your foot flexed to help!

3. You absolutely want to cross the fabric and wrap it one more time around the ankle.

tip If you do not do this you greatly increase your chances of falling out.

REMINDER:

Remember to be super mindful of your ankle wrap. There is possibility of the wrap coming undone, however double wrapping will help!

RELEASE LOWER LEG

GET LOTS OF FABRIC SLACK FIRST

DO A SINGLE FOOTLOCK ON BOTH TAIL TOGETHER

PUSH FABRIC OUT AND LIFT CHEST UP

4. Once you feel your ankle is secure, release your lower leg from its footlock.

> !tip Hold on tightly to the fabric during this process, this is a great way to "feel" out your ankle wraps security.

5. You then want to lift up the tails and get ALOT of slack.

> !tip The more the better, there is a good chance you may have to redo this part a couple times until you get used to how much slack you need to actualy get into the pose.

6. Once you get slack do a single footlock on that tail.
7. From there begin to push out the fabric and slide your chest upright.

> !tip Think about swivelling the hips, rotating so the "back" leg is behind you in the air. Arch your back and push the fabric away from you.

83. BOUND BALLERINA ⚠️

FROM A WRIST WRAP IN BELAY

REMINDER:

The Bound Ballerina is extremely intense on the shoulders! I recommend having a good shoulder warm up beforehand. TO EXIT: You need to reverse back the way you came. Crunch into a ball and drive your booty back up and over the tails.

tip

Keep in mind the closer your hands are toward each other the more intense the pose becomes. Try it a few times with your lower hand between shoulder and hip level.

START IN WRIST WRAP AND FREE HANGING LEGS

KNEES COME UP AND OVER BOTTOM HAND

FLEX FEET AND CATCH ON FABRIC

RELEASE TOP LEG

1. From a Belay Loop, footlock around both tails. Slide your body through the loop until you have just your wrist left wrapped in the loop.
2. Release your legs so that you are in a wrist hang with your free arm holding onto both tails together.

tip Like the first image above. Remember the closer your hands are towards each other the harder the pose becomes.

3. Bring both knees up to your hand holding the tails and slide your knees OVER that hand and through. Flex your feet to catch on the tails.
4. Push against the tail/arch your back. Release your TOP LEG down towards ground.
5. Extend and arch into a split.

⚠️ Losing your grip or extending to far into the pose are both issues that can cause you to fall or get injured.

CHAPTER SIX
MISCELLANEOUS POSES

Welcome to Chapter Six, here you will find poses with unique entries. Bear in mind that unique entries can also push the body in new ways. Always warm up before practicing!

pg 118

pg 120

pg 121

pg 122

pg 124

pg 125

pg 126

pg 128

84. MIDDLE SPLIT BALANCE

FROM A TRIPLE WRAP

This balance split works best from a triple wrap. But does have potential for sliding out. Sink into your triple wraps to get them tight. Sliding can also be due to a particular legging or even the weather if you are training in cold environments.

REMINDER:

This pose is also very taxing on your hamstrings and groin area so be sure to thoroughly warm up and practice hamstring/groin exercises to strengthen yourself for this pose!

OPEN LEGS BEHIND FABRIC

BEND LEGS OVER FABRIC

BRING THEM BEHIND AND THEN OUT TO THE SIDE AGAIN

1. For this pose you will be wrapping your lower legs around the fabric 3 times total.
2. Lift your body and straddle your legs BEHIND the fabric.
3. Bend your legs over and to the front of the fabric.
4. Feed your ankles between the poles, behind you and then out to the side.

(tip) All this creates one giant circular motion with your lower legs that wraps the fabric around them.

pg 118

5. Repeat this process 2 more times until you have wrapped a total of 3 times.

WRAP TAILS 3 TMIES

6. After you complete your 3rd wrap close your legs together and sink your weight into the wraps to tighten them around the ankles.

PUSH DOWN INTO WRAPS TO TIGHTEN THEM

OPEN INTO MIDDLE SPLIT

PRESS ARMS AGAINST POLES TO HELP BALANCE

7. From there simply open your legs into a straddle and bring your chest and arms to the front.

tip

To do a true balance you want to adjust your body positioning slightly. Close your legs together into a very slight V shape, drop your booty back behind you more, and lean your chest and arms forward.

85. FRONT SPLIT BALANCE
FROM A TRIPLE WRAP

REMINDER:

The same as with Middle Balance, make sure your ankles are wrapped nice and tight. Warm up properly and exercise the hammies and groin to gain balance strength!

PUSH DOWN INTO THE WRAP TO TIGHTEN

OPEN INTO FRONT SPLIT

1. To enter follow all the steps for Middle Split Balance (pg 118)
2. Once your wraps are tightened open your legs, turn your hip through and spread into a full split!

REMINDER:

This is another big balancing act that requires lots of core, hamstring, groin and thigh strength. Your back leg thigh is pushing down into the fabric, your front leg hamstring is pushing down and squeezing onto the fabric and your core and arms are helping to achieve the proper balancing point!

86. KNEE TANGLE SPLIT
FROM A TRIPLE WRAP ON ONE LEG

REMINDER:
Split from a triple wrap! This one is also about balance so don't forget to enter slowly and controlled!

Go SLOWLY into this split. It is extremly easy to tip over the other end if you extend too fast.

- TRIPLE WRAP BOTH POLES ONTO ONE LEG
- SPLIT THE POLES
- FOLD THROUGH
- FREE LEG PASSES UP THROUGH POLES AND INTO A SPLIT

1. Triple wrap your right leg. Both poles are together on just one leg.
2. While keeping your wrap secure split the poles and forward fold through.
3. Hold onto your poles about hip level with your thumbs facing up.
4. Lift your free leg up to the ceiling and then pass it through the poles into a split.
5. Be mindful of over rotating!

pg 121

87. CREATURE SPLIT
FROM A TRIPLE LEG WRAP WITHOUT FOOTLOCK

tip

The trick with this pose is to keep as much tension on your tails as possible and try to swing your legs around as wide as possible. This one may take some time as most people tend to slip back into a bent knee hang.

OPEN LEGS BEHIND FABRIC

BEND LEGS OVER FABRIC

BRING THEM BEHIND AND THEN OUT TO THE SIDE AGAIN

1. For this pose you will be wrapping your lower legs around the fabric 3 times total.
2. Lift your body and straddle your legs BEHIND the fabric.
3. Bend your legs over and to the front of the fabric.
4. Feed your ankles between the poles, behind you and then out to the side.
5. Repeat this process 2 more times until you have wrapped a total of 3 times and then squeeze your ankles together.

SQUEEZE ANKLES TOGETHER AFTER 3 WRAPS

6. Keep your legs squeezed together, bring your chest through the poles and forward fold.

(tip) Allow the fabric to slip under the hip bones.

7. Once folded grab each tail in each hand. Right tail in right hand and left tail in left hand.
8. Hold tightly onto the tails and begin to split your legs in a wide straddle.

You MUST pull down hard on the tails as you swing your legs

9. Bring your legs out to the side in a wide straddle, as wide as possible. Drive your legs around the side and then over your head in an arch.
10. You want so much tension on the tails it almost feels like you can't get your legs around.

(tip) Remember the legs must straddle wide. You want them to rotate to the side as much as possible and not over your head.

BRING FREE TAIL FORWARD INTO A SPLIT

SWITCH GRIP TO ONE TAIL

KEEP ALOT OF TENSION ON THIS TAIL

11. Arch your back as much as possible and walk your hands up the tails.

12. Switch both hands to one fabric tail. (tip) Keep as much tension on the fabric as possible.

13. Hold the tension in that tail and keep your leg squeezed as straight as possible.
14. Begin to pass the free leg around towards the front of your body so it is pointing away from your stomach and you are in an upside down split position.
15. The biggest thing here is to pull down tightly on your back leg fabric tail and keep as much tension there as possible.

88. BALLERINA

FROM A SINGLE ARM CROCHETE

⚠️ This pose requires a great amount of grip and wrist strength. If your top arm slips and falls to the other side of the pole you will fall.

💡 *tip* When wrapping your base arm be sure to have your thumb pointing down and keep your arm pulled in close to your body.

1. From a climb, crochete your body around the pole.

   💡 *tip* If you want your base arm to be your right arm then slide your body to the left side of the pole as you crochete around.

NO FOOTLOCK JUST A CLIMB

CROCHETE YOUR BODY TO THE LEFT AND AROUND THE FABRIC

RE-GRIP SO YOUR LEFT ARM IS OVER THE FABRIC

3. After you get your left arm repositioned, slide your hips out to the left side as well so you can look down and see the bottom pole of the fabric.

CROCHETE RIGHT ARM ON BOTTOM POLE

RELEASE LEGS

GRIP BACK LEG WITH SAME SIDE HAND

EXTEND

DRIVE ARM DOWN

4. Crochete your bottom arm (from the outside in) around the bottom pole of the fabric.
5. Straighten/strengthen your arm and release your feet from the fabric.
6. Grab your left ankle with your top left arm and extend into a dancer split.
7. Simultaneously squeeze your right arm in and point it down to the ground.

89. BOUND BALLERINA
FROM A HAND HANG GRIP

REMINDER:
Choosing the best hand grip and lower arm placement is key on making this pose work for you. See the tips below for hand placement help.

The fall potential comes from losing your grip

CROCHETE OR USE A NORMAL HAND HANG GRIP

THUMB FACING UP

BOTH KNEES COME UP AND OVER BOTTOM ARM

FLEX YOUR FEET TO CATCH ON FABRIC AS YOU GO THROUGH

1. From a climbing position, squat down slightly and reach your strong arm up high.

tip You can do this from a footlock but its best to just hold the fabric between your feet.

2. Either crochete your strong arm above your head OR hold the pole with a normal hand grip.

tip The crochete can bother your wrists but some people feel more grip security in the crochete.

3. With the bottom arm grip the fabric thumb facing UP about hip height.

tip A higher grip makes the pose and entry harder. Lower grip makes the pose and entry easier.

4. Release your legs and bring both knees up and over the bottom arm in between the fabric. Flex your feet to catch against the fabric.

5. As you bring your knees through catch both feet against the fabric.
6. Release the TOP leg and point it to the floor.
7. Keep the other leg hooked in and push into the tail, extend and split as much as you can.

BOTH KNEES COME OVER AND THROUGH

KEEP BOTTOM FOOT HOOKED IN FABRIC

RELEASE TOP LEG THROUGH

POINT FREE LEG DOWN AND PUSH THROUGH BACK LEG INTO A SPLIT

pg 125

90. HIP KEY SPLIT ⚠️

FROM A HIP KEY

⚠️ This wrap is not a secure hold. If you let go of your tail once in the pose, there is a huge chance you could slide out. SOMETIMES if the wrap is tight enough or leggings sticky enough it will hold and you can let go. HOWEVER this is not a guaranteed hold. Practice carefully.

REMINDER:
TO EXIT: You need to reverse the steps. Bend your top knee, pull yourself back up and key over into your hip key. Pay attention to which side of the pole you bend your knee over. It needs to be the same side as the initial start.

HIP KEY

SCOOT TAIL UP TO LOWER BACK

1. Complete a full hip key. Shown above.
2. Once keyed over, scoot the tail up above your booty and rest on lower back.

TAIL OVER LOWER BACK — GRAB TAIL — TOSS TAIL BETWEEN LEGS — REGRIP TAIL UNDER THIGH — BRING LEGS TOGETHER

3. With your bottom hand, grab the tail and toss it between your legs.
4. Regrip the tail by reaching under your bottom leg and cinching up any slack.

5. Hold tightly to your tail, lower your booty to the floor and bend your wrapped knee.

> **tip:** You are essentialy falling out of your hip key, however the extra tail wrap will cinch around your bent knee and lock you in.

DROP YOUR BOOTY TO THE FLOOR AND BEND YOUR WRAPPED KNEE

HOLD TIGHT TO YOUR TAIL

HOLD TIGHT TO YOUR TAIL AND DROP CHEST TO INVERT

OPEN TOP LEG INTO A SPLIT

6. Lower your chest down into an inversion.
7. Extend top leg into a split.

⚠️ Remember to hold onto your tail or you could fall.

pg 127

91. ANKLE HANG TRIANGLE SPLIT ⚠️

FROM A SINGLE ANKLE HANG

REMINDER:

This pose can be painful on your ankle. You should be extremely comfortable in regular single ankle hangs before working this pose. I have also found this pose is easier on high stretch fabric. TO EXIT: release your bottom leg footlock, reach back up for your ankle and pull up into a squat or stand.

1. Double wrap the tail around your right foot.
2. Lean back and begin to lower your body down.
As you do this the tails will begin to cinch up by your ankle.

DOUBLE WRAP

SLIDE BODY DOWN

ANKLE CATCHES AGAINST POLE

FREE FOOT FORWARD

GET SLACK AND FOOTLOCK

3. Flex your right foot and once lowered all the way let your right foot catch against the outer or left side of the pole.

⚠️ The side in which you catch is very important. There is fall potential if you are not mindful.

4. Once in your ankle hang, lower all the way down and bring your free foot forward.
5. Bring up the slack on your tail and use it to do a footlock on your free leg.

tip You will need ALOT of slack for this pose. Finding the exact amount can be a learning curve, you can learn to keep track of how much slack you need by counting how many "arm pulls" are required to perform the pose. An arm pull would be you reaching as low as you can on the tail and then pulling it up to your chest.

pg 128

5. Rotate chest and body outward 180 degrees.
6. Place your shoulder into the slack and begin to push the slack out forwards.
7. Walk your hands up the slack as much as possible and extend into a split.

Printed in Great Britain
by Amazon